Start and Grow Profitable Business

Operate Your Own Profitable Cleaning Business

(Learn How to Make Money by Teaching and Selling Your Online Class)

Millie Bruce

Published By **Darby Connor**

Millie Bruce

Start and Grow Profitable Business: Operate Your Own Profitable Cleaning Business (Learn How to Make Money by Teaching and Selling Your Online Class)

ISBN 978-1-77485-705-2

No part of this guidebook shall be reproduced in any form without permission in writing from the publisher except in the case of brief quotations embodied in critical articles or reviews.

Legal & Disclaimer

The information contained in this ebook is not designed to replace or take the place of any form of medicine or professional medical advice. The information in this ebook has been provided for educational & entertainment purposes only.

The information contained in this book has been compiled from sources deemed reliable, and it is accurate to the best of the Author's knowledge; however, the Author cannot guarantee its accuracy and validity and cannot be held liable for any errors or omissions. Changes are periodically made to this book. You must consult your doctor or get professional medical advice before using any of the suggested remedies, techniques, or information in this book.

Upon using the information contained in this book, you agree to hold harmless the Author from and against any damages, costs, and expenses, including any legal fees potentially resulting from the application of any of the information provided by this guide. This disclaimer applies to any damages or injury caused by the use and application, whether directly or indirectly, of any advice or information presented, whether for breach of contract, tort, negligence, personal injury, criminal intent, or under any other cause of action.

You agree to accept all risks of using the information presented inside this book. You need to consult a professional medical practitioner in order to ensure you are both able and healthy enough to participate in this program.

TABLE OF CONTENTS

Introduction

If you're looking to create a company starting a small company, a small one might be the ideal method to achieve it. But what exactly is a small company? How can you tell whether your idea can be successful in the business world of small businesses? Once you've established what can you do to grow into a large-scale company?

Its Small Business Startup guide has everything you require to become a small-business owner. This guide will discuss the essentials of a small-sized business and provide a variety of alternatives for structuring your business. We'll go over all the legal issues to consider prior to making the leap from an employee to an owner of a small-sized business. We'll discuss how to start your business with a solid plan to establish relationships with your customers and expand massively. In the final part, we'll discuss methods to grow the business of your company to accommodate increasing needs.

This book will assist you in starting your business in the right direction. Begin this journey with us and, in the near future you'll have the tools you need for success in small-scale business. The key to success are within your control and this guide will give you the tools you need - and teaches you how to apply these tools. To make your business idea be successful, it has to be financially viable. There are many options for businesses to earn money.

This guide will help you in investigating the various types of companies and determining the most profitable one that is right for you. We'll take you on the journey through various possible small business models. Most importantly we'll go over ways you can manage your startup's financials in order.

The information contained in this guide applies to all types of small-scale business startup that include restaurants, stores for retail and eCommerce companies. Beginning a small-scale company isn't an easy task. It's actually one of the most difficult decisions you'll ever undertake. If you're considering moving between "employed" and "entrepreneur," this Small Business Startup guide will assist you throughout the process.

Your business's concept is the thing that will help you achieve your goals. Even if you're planning on hiring others to help you It's still your concept. In this guide we'll discuss different kinds of businesses. Keep in mind that what's suitable for one business owner may not be suitable for someone else, which is why it's essential to conduct your own research prior to making any major decision.

Let this guide illuminate the way to plan your company's growth. The model of business you select and the marketing strategy you create will provide an outline of your route towards entrepreneurship. If you've decided to make the leap and begin your own business This guide will assist you in laying solid foundations for it. Although every business is unique and there's no set method to success By following these first steps, you'll be on the way to establishing an organization that is a reflection of your personality as an businessperson!

Chapter 1: The Profitable Idea

"Profit isn't the primary reason for business. The reason for the business is to provide an item or service customers require and to do it efficiently enough to make it profitable."
James Rouse James Rouse

Small-scale business startups are the most profitable venture you can ever accomplish. It's not easy and sacrifice, but that's the reason that makes it so satisfying. If you are employed by an employer your time and efforts are rewarded depending on how much someone's able for you to be paid. If they aren't satisfied with your results, they'll dismiss you and then hire an employee who is new. If you run your own company your time is compensated according to the rates you choose to set. The amount you pay for your time is only in the direction of the amount of effort you choose to invest in it. The earnings are all yours.

There's no guarantee that you will succeed however, a small-scale business start-up is the most lucrative chance to earn a fortune and make a living as a boss. It's hard to beat the excitement when you build an enterprise from the ground from scratch and earning money from what you've built. But, there are a number of aspects that small business startup companies must be considered prior to launching one. This chapter will walk you through the process of conceptualizing and imagining an effective business. We'll go over the niches that generate the most profits and how to pick which one is right for you and your company.

Conceptualization and Ideation

The process of converting an idea to being rich is long and complex to conceptualize an idea. will lead you down a variety of avenues. It is important to consider each of these prior to deciding to decide to take any action. In the beginning, you must identify a problem that could be addressed in a way that nobody previously thought of, or find a solution to a challenge that other people have attempted to solve but have failed. You must then convert your idea into a successful business. The method should be similar to this:

1. Brainstorming

Brainstorming is the method of creating as many ideas as you can. There are a variety of methods to brainstorming, like the use of sticky notes making diagrams on a whiteboard with index cards or even discussing it with your fellow classmates. Whatever method you choose to use for it, you must take all of your ideas out in a format prior to deciding which ones are worthy of further exploration.

Record as many thoughts that you are able to, no matter how absurd or unlogical they may appear. It's impossible to know which can lead to a profitable business plan. Don't make any judgments yet. Whatever crazy or absurd that might be, one of these ideas could be the foundation for a profitable business.

2. Sorting through Your Thoughts

When the list are finished, you can reduce them to the feasibility of them. This is a process that requires contemplation and lots of study. It is essential to understand everything you can about your thoughts. It's not enough just to believe you're an expert on the subject. Learn from publications, watch videos and attend classes or seminars and speak with successful business owners or entrepreneurs in your community with the exact that you are.

3. Making Your Business Model

After weighing your thoughts and your research Write down the advantages and disadvantages of each. Which has the greatest advantages? Which is likely to cause the largest number of problems? Consider comparing every advantage to every issue. If pros outweigh cons this is how you can determine what is the most effective option. It's not possible to be perfect in this. It's difficult to predict every single benefit or consequence associated with an concept. Simply do your best and pray for the most favorable outcome. After you've decided on your business model, it's the time to take the first step towards making that plan an actual business that is profitable.

What is the most profitable way to market your idea?

Before you begin your business it is crucial to determine what you can do to make your idea profitable. Consider, for instance, the number of people taking to Kickstarter to help fund their latest ideas. They're aware of the market for the product they're trying to create.

If you are considering this, be sure that you consider more than the initial process of ideation and conceptualization. It's not enough to have your idea to simply be tempting. Consider ways to implement this idea in real-world issues, either through an actual product or a an approach that is based on services.

The final part is crucial because you'll need to design an actual product to sell or provide a service that customers would be willing to purchase. You might think you've got an incredible idea, but no one would want to invest their money on something that isn't able to solve any issues!

When you're creating a product it is more important to have enough funds to start your company off on the starting point, since you'll have to purchase equipment and supplies, as well as research the type of equipment that best fits your needs.

Niche Markets

Every business requires an audience that's big enough to make a profit. The trick is to determine precisely where people are interested in to buy what you're selling, and to purchase it. This is where the idea of the niche market comes into play.

Although it may sell a variety of products, every company has a segment of market. Every item or service should be offered to a specific kind of person or group of people. It's easier to explain this with an example, such as the pet industry, which sells products for cats, dogs as well as rabbits, fish even snakes and Lizards. Every person in this market is searching for something unique as everyone wants the pets they love to stay content and healthy. The pet owners make up the primary market that we are in, with every type of pet owner seeking something unique according to the needs of their pet.

Some markets are more populated than other markets, and their competition is fierce. However, there can some markets that aren't big or competitive, which makes them ideal for small-scale businesses since there's plenty of room for grow and it doesn't take long to become established. Here are some examples of niche markets that can be profitable:

1. Beauty Products, Makeup and Beauty Products

This is a huge industry for both women and men. It's over-saturated in larger cities, where a lot of people are proud of their appearance and take on a crowd that is that is obsessed with appearances. All except the smaller towns, where people wear makeup less frequently but it's still a great market to explore since it takes a short time to establish a following.

2. Home-based Business Ideas

This is a hugely well-known niche market that is ideal to local marketing through network events as well as referrals. People will buy from a person they know personally and so getting them be aware of you is the key. This market is ideal for the home-based bakery which can be marketed to mothers who require birthday cakes or birthday party favors. wedding cakes, as well as custom cookies for special occasions.

3. High-Profit Items

This is a market segment that refers to products that are highly sought-after and require only a modest increase from wholesale prices. They can also need a substantial amount of startup capital, therefore they're not suitable for every company and are typically for established companies looking to increase the channels of sales. One example is selling perfume in department stores with high-end prices in which there is a chance to make profits despite the costly wholesale prices.

4. High-End Services

Services are everywhere. That can be the reason the highest-profit are those that require an enormous amount of money, yet can yield amazing earnings. An excellent example is the development of software. It's costly to create custom software, however it's easy to market it to various customers once it's completed.

5. Small Business Marketing

SMB marketing is among the most sought-after niches in the present. It's a great option for consulting or SEO testing, where there are plenty of opportunities to earn money, even with very few customers. It's only a matter of the time and effort to establish relationships with clients in order to be profitable, even with a lot of competitors.

While they're all excellent niche markets, some aren't worth pursuing because they're not competitive enough to sustain a company. This includes any market which demands that the item or product to be of broad appeal in order to make money. For instance selling a common clothes line or household item will require much more capital than a smaller business could afford, which makes it difficult to start.

If you're not certain which type of business you want to launch. In this situation, there's many other niche markets that are easy to enter because they don't require any investment or time to establish your reputation. Here are five of them:

6. Recycled Items

Selling items that are used is a simple business idea that anyone could turn into a lucrative venture even if it becomes a hobby selling the items on a couple of websites. One of the best examples is selling your old clothes and giving the proceeds to charities, or rehabilitating old electronic equipment, or even supplies for parties and events, and then selling them for an increase.

7. Babysitting

This is a great opportunity to turn something that you enjoy into a lucrative business. It will require very little initial capital. It is easy to gain clients through word of mouth, particularly when you've got certificates regarding things like CPR as well as first-aid.

8. Physical Services

Physical services are things like haircuts, manicures, and manicures that can be listed on Craigslist or via the word-of-mouth. These are typically skills that require less capital investment than such as home remodeling or construction since there's no requirement to buy equipment that isn't needed or to hire staff.

9. Online Sales

Participating in the e-commerce market is fairly simple. A lot of popular websites can connect buyers with independent sellers However, it's extremely difficult to break into due to the large numerous successful stores that are that are already in operation. It is best to stay clear of this market until you're certain that you'll make a mark.

10. Crafts

Crafting unique items is another fantastic way to transform your passion into a lucrative business. It requires only a small amount of investment capital since only a few items are needed to start. With the proper marketing strategy many people will purchase your products.

Although all of them are excellent alternatives, one is fast becoming extremely popular because it's able to operated from your personal home. It's selling services on the internet. This kind of business permits freelancers to take on clients via easy-to-use websites such as Fiverr as well as Upwork.

How Competition Impacts Your Startup

The choice of whether or not you go into an area that has a lot of competitors can significantly impact your profits. You might have a great idea but in the event that there are many similar companies operating in your locality It will be more difficult to make it financially successful.

The most effective way to accomplish this is to do it through advertising and service to customers. For instance, if you're selling a product it is essential to create an original twist to ensure that your company stands out from the rest of the competitors. If you're operating a business that is based on service that you offer services at a reasonable price or be extremely flexible.

Digital or Tangible Product

There are two options to manage a successful business. What you want to achieve with your product's physical or electronic, can determine either.

Customer-Oriented

The most effective type of company is one that meets the requirements of customers or provides them with something that they didn't know they needed. If your market is one that has many competitors or not is another factor to take into consideration as it will determine the speed at which you will achieve success.

One of the best examples are fashion labels and retail stores that focus on aesthetics, such as clothing for infants or women who adore 1920s fashion. Smaller businesses that offer more items such as books, gifts or other items might need to set up an office space regardless of whether they plan to sell on the internet.

Service-Oriented

If you have a product or service to provide that meets an interest or need in your clients, this is the best business model as it does not require the same amount of capital that the purchase of a tangible item could. Depending on the type of service you provide it is possible to advertise your service by word of mouth and/or websites such as Craigslist or Fiverr. Examples include babysitting, physical education, graphic design, modeling and catering. They can also be customized to specific niches, based on the marketplace you're targeting.

If you decide to go with the option of tangible products take note that this could mean greater startup capital and time to build your business as you'll need money to purchase the supplies you need for your products prior to when you are able to begin selling them.

Take into consideration whether your business is the best fit for tangible goods or services. The former requires greater capital to start since you'll require all the equipment you need prior to doing any other thing. But, the second alternative will require less time and more cash upfront, but is still profitable.

These products are ideal for people who wish to sell their brands because it requires longer and more money to start and requires an establishment with a storefront. But, this type of type of product is ideal for people who have unique ideas on the improvement of standard products like clothes and materials.

Most important to keep in mind when trying to create an income-generating company is that if aren't equipped with the right abilities the chances of succeeding are drastically reduced. Try to reverse engineer your concept by considering the required capabilities for your idea before deciding whether it's something you're skilled in - or you can train yourself to master.

You should only go after the type of business that matches your interests and aspirations. The most important thing is to start an enterprise that you aren't really passionate about since it's unlikely to succeed for long. It is also important to research the location you'll be working in and determine if there's lots of competition. The location of your business will determine its growth and success, as will the amount of time and cash you'll require prior to even getting up and running.

Chapter 2: Selecting An Appropriate

Business Model

Before you start the thrilling process of starting your own small-scale business, you must to figure out which business model is the best for your needs. Be aware that there are many variations of each model and hybrids are also possible. However most successful companies fall in one of these types of models.

The choice you make will impact the types of customers you are targeting, the amount of cash you'll need in order to begin as well as whether you are officially included. This chapter will focus on the brick-and-mortar model of business and the home-based model. It will also discuss the benefits of small company ownership, and what each model's pros and cons are weighed against.

Brick-and-Mortar

Brick-and-mortar (or storefront) firm is one which has physical presence in the local community regardless of whether it's an office space or a storefront. A variety of businesses be considered to fall into this category such as department shops, grocery stores bakeries, clothing stores, and even restaurants. These establishments have physical locations in which you can buy their products or services. Customers come to the shop to browse the selection. The employees are there to help with questions and take payments.

The brick-and-mortar model of business has been in use for centuries and is still an increasingly popular choice for businesses due to its flexibility and simplicity of use. It doesn't require particular software or technology to operate, meaning you do not need to invest cash on computers or equipment. It is possible to choose the area based on the number of people within your neighborhood or wherever you think is most convenient to customers. You can also pick the size of space you require for your storefront, whether it's a tiny one or a massive warehouse.

There are some disadvantages for this type of business. Brick-and-mortar stores require inventory and staff to operate efficiently. There's a significant amount of expense that comes with leasing or buying an area and stocking stocks. A lot of brick and mortar stores require employees to manage the business and assist customers with queries, meaning they will need to pay for them. This can be a substantial amount of dollars. There could be an increase in costs if your company experiences seasonal fluctuations and sells specific items only during specific dates during the course of the calendar year.

As well as these disadvantages in addition, you'll need to address compliance issues when you start an organization. It is possible that you will need an approval for zoning, sign an agreement to lease and request an exemption from sales tax from the government. You will need to spend time and funds upfront before the store opens.

Advantages of Brick-and mortar Businesses

* You're in the same community that your customers are, which makes it easier to promote your company.

Your overhead costs are usually less than that of an online company because you don't have to purchase equipment or software.

* Customers enjoy shopping in person since they can ask questions and look at the items they would like to buy.

It's simpler and cheaper to manage compliance issues in a brick and mortar business than it is in an online-based business.

* You can market your services and products face-to-face with your clients and create an impression.

The negatives of brick-and-mortar businesses

It can be costly to lease or buy an office space and pay employees. It is also possible to experience delays when your business isn't generating any revenues.

Employees are required to be compensated to keep the business efficiently - an additional cost when the business hasn't been generating any revenue.

If you're operating in a seasonal business it is necessary to pay employees all year long even if your company isn't in operation.

It's much more difficult to be able to respond rapidly to customers who visit your shop or at your place of business.

There is a chance that you will be the victim of burglary and theft. You'll need insurance to safeguard yourself in the event that such events occur because you handle valuable cash and inventory in the premises.

Work-From-Home

The work-from-home or online business model is exactly what it looks like. There's no brick-and-mortar store, but you market your services and products to potential customers using online platforms such as Amazon FBA, Shopify, and BigCommerce. So, you can manage your business from any place connected to the internet. There is no need to fret about the operating expenses, like rent and utilities for a shopfront. It is not necessary to have an actual location for your business.

The absence of overhead costs makes operating an online business cheaper than a brick and mortar store. It won't have the costs associated with leasing or buying a business and stocking your inventory, meaning you can save money on these cost-of-living expenses. However, your clients won't be able to visit your establishment and engage with you personally.

The main drawback of this method is that your customers are limited to people with internet access. This can impact sales based on the market you intend to target. There is also the possibility of increased costs based on the shipping options you select for your items in particular if you offer large or bulky products.

This is a practical model and convenient, however it is flexible, and lets you set your work hours depending on your timetable. It allows you to balance obligations to your family and work without having to compromise one to make room for the other as it is easy to alter your schedule according to. Furthermore, this approach is ideal for people who are having a hard time finding work or require a second source of source of income. You'll have complete control over the amount of money you make through your products as well as the time you put into your business, as well as the amount of work you devote to it.

If you invest the effort and time required to manage your business effectively you could earn significant profits. There are however a few aspects to think about before you commit to this type of business. Here are some advantages and disadvantages of the work-from-home or online option that you need to think about before deciding if it is the right choice for your company idea.

The pros of work-from-home businesses

* You don't have to worry about the stress and cost of buying or renting the space.

The sky is the limit on the amount you can earn as you have total control of the price and choice of products.

* You don't need more employees to manage your business well.

* You are able to be as busy or as lightly as you'd want.

* There's no downtime as the only thing that can limit your business is your imagination , and determination to achieve success.

The pros and cons of working from home businesses

Customers must have access to the internet to make purchases from you. This severely restricts the number of customers you have and could influence sales.

* You need to have reliable and reliable internet connectivity for your business to run it successfully.

There isn't a physical location where you can meet with customers and talk to them in person.

Customers are not allowed to touch and feel the products they purchase.

The choice of a business model

The work-from-home or online business model is perfect for those who require flexibility in their work schedules and are confident about attracting customers. However, this business model demands more work from the business owner than a brick-and-mortar shop like the marketing aspect and providing customer services. Brick-and-mortar businesses are more costly to begin and maintain. However, it is a benefit to have the physical presence of a storefront or place where customers can talk to the company or its products in person.

It is essential to evaluate the amount of effort you're willing to put into your company before you decide on a strategy.

You might also wish to think about the location you'd like to work from. In particular, an internet-based or work-from home model is ideal for those living in areas with a lot of rurality where brick and mortar stores are not plentiful and are an expense. A physical storefront could be more feasible in areas that have a high population density.

Furthermore, you must take into consideration your customer base and what they'd like to see. Most of your customers have access to the internet, but when the majority of your clientele isn't or comes from a region where brick-and-mortar establishments are the norm, then the physical location could be ideal for your needs. The type of model you select will be contingent on a variety of factors however it is advantageous to explore both models to be successful.

The difference between an online and Brick-and-Mortar-based Business

The most significant distinction between an online-based business and brick-and-mortar locations is the level of convenience and control that you have over your working hours. A business that is online caters to those shopping online. This is which can increase sales as most customers don't prefer brick-and-mortar stores. It is possible to conduct your entire business online without the need to establish any physical premises. Additionally, you will not be liable for costs such as electricity and rent while conducting your business online since you don't manage or own an actual store.

However you can have complete control over your working schedule in a brick and mortar location as your business is based out of an actual place. You can get the most of this by being able to open your business at any time you'd like, which is great if you have a job or a career that has specific times. In addition, you don't need to employ employees to manage your business since it will be run and managed by one person, which is you.

But suppose that your target customers are online and do not visit brick-and-mortar stores. In this situation, you might prefer to establish an online company instead of having a physical shop. Furthermore, the expense of opening a brick and mortar business can be difficult for those who have limited funds.

The work-from-home, or online-based business model could be the best for those who are flexible in their working schedules and have experience in marketing, building a solid base of customers, and delivering outstanding customer service because it allows you to control how much effort you would like to devote to your business. But, it is important to not overlook the advantages of having a physical shopfront for your company. It's beneficial to combine both strategies to increase potential for success.

What is the most Lucrative are Online Business?

A well-established online presence could be extremely profitable for many business owners, however it is contingent on the kind of products or services that you offer. If, for instance, you're an industry expert, and write articles or provide consultation services, it is likely to result in a profitable ROI on time as well as invested. But, if you're far from being an authority in your area or do not have a following through social media platforms, it might be difficult to make it.

If your field of expertise is not available online, you'll have to develop the product on your own. Through an online company you are able to reach people across the world and offer them something that isn't readily accessible, like the physical item as well as a personal one. For example, successful entrepreneurs design and sell books, software music, art or even jewellery.

If you are considering starting an online company but you don't have the know-how. If that's the scenario, you'll have to outsource or obtain assistance from others in order to develop your product. If you do not have a significant fan base on social platforms, or don't know how to promote your product efficiently then you'll need to fund paid advertising campaigns, like Google Adwords - to promote your business and connect with potential customers.

Your success in an online business will depend on how well you promote the product you offer or services. If you're not a pro in marketing hiring someone with enough experience to guide you is a smart move. If you're thinking of beginning an online business, this is the ideal time since there are numerous choices to pick from.

Dropshipping

Dropshipping is an established model of business used by people operating online stores. It is a great option for people lacking the money to buy inventory. This model lets you buy items from manufacturers or wholesalers, and then sell them to your customers (with the addition of a markup). When you earn a profit and you are able to purchase the product on behalf of your customer and then deliver the item direct to them. After you receive the money then you repay your supplier.

Amazon FBA

This kind approach to business have grown in popularity, especially in the past few years. In this instance you utilize Amazon as your shop and you ship your entire inventory into the Amazon warehouse. If someone buys via you Amazon delivers the goods for you and notifies you when the product is delivered. Then, you pay for these services. But nonetheless, you get the benefit of selling your goods on Amazon's website, which attracts millions of customers each day!

Self-Publishing

If you're in the know in your area, but do not have the funds needed to create an ebook or create programs, there is a different method of developing your product. Self-publishing lets you create and publish content on websites that have gained significant followings, with specific readerships. Once your content is published, you retain up 70% to 70% of earnings, and can make use of these profits to invest in your company.

An online business can be extremely lucrative however, it is contingent on the kind of products or services you offer. People who are experts in certain subjects should make the most of this by writing pieces or creating material that could be utilized for other uses like e-books, podcasts, or other kind of media. If you own an online company you're the boss, and you can choose of working from your home, or spend longer with family. It's the right opportunity to make the very first leap into the lucrative industry since there are many options open to those looking to establish their own business.

There are a myriad of methods to begin your own online company, regardless of your experience there will be an opportunity to create products or services. The most important thing is the way you promote your product, as well as the amount you spend on marketing campaigns as well as other types of marketing. There must be new products available to keep customers returning. This ensures that you earn more sales and will also get regular business.

The time is now to begin the small-scale business. It doesn't matter whether you have plenty of knowledge in marketing or not. It is possible to employ experts to assist you by making use of the large variety of freelance sites online to save money, while hopefully , ensuring the success of your business.

Chapter 3: The Legal Considerations

Small-scale businesses are prevalent across the globe. Many people have dreams of starting their own business, however most will not make it beyond the initial planning phase. A few will fail because they didn't conduct enough research. Other are unable to succeed because competitors were too formidable to manage.

Whatever group you fall in regardless of your position, it is essential to remain calm. It is an ideal idea to seek out an associate of the company, or at a minimum, an advisor for more precise feedback on the potential of your business concept and also legal advice throughout the process. Legal issues are particularly important for those looking to incorporate their business into a intend to become entrepreneurs. This chapter will guide you through the fundamentals regarding each type of legal entity as well as its benefits and drawbacks.

Sole Proprietorship

Being sole proprietorship is by far the most straightforward way to start your own business. It is possible to begin selling products or services without being held up by bureaucracy and large amount of paperwork. It is possible to check with your local government office or the state's website for business to determine whether you have to establish a company. In general, the more complicated your business model is as well as the greater formalities that you would like to incorporate (such such as holding an annual General Meeting for shareholders) and the more complicated it will have to be legal.

It is simple to run a sole proprietorship as you don't have to be concerned with the same legal requirements as you would in a corporate environment such as choosing officers, the multitude of required reports and filings and holding annual meetings. In the majority of US states, you'll be legally obliged to file the final tax returns and VAT returns. in the UK, Australia, and the EU have similar regulations that you should make sure to check with the local office for business registration to fulfill other legal obligations.

Benefits of Sole Proprietorship

* There aren't any requirements for capital minimums, which means you won't be required to pay money prior to starting.

* You can begin your business in just a few moments by opening an account at a bank in its name and purchasing the required equipment.

If you opt to buy your own business it'll be a breeze.

A sole proprietor isn't taxed as an independent entity. So, they don't have to have to pay taxes like a business However, personal income taxes have to be paid.

* You don't have to apply for incorporation or other similar legal procedures that are burdensome.

The disadvantages of sole proprietorship

If you are sued, your assets could be at risk.

* You are required to pay tax on the income from your business since it's not recorded in your books.

* You personally are responsible for any business-related debts that your company incurs.

Taxes are due on every cent of business earnings and you are not able to choose to pay tax on gross or net receipts.

* There isn't a separate owner's equity.

Corporation/C Corp

A company has the status of a legal person, with rights as well as privileges and liabilities. It is possible to sign contracts on behalf of your business and you don't need to take on personal debt. You can, for instance, purchase assets under the name of your company without penalties. While this might sound great but there's drawbacks. Before we look, let's take a take a look at the upsides!

Benefits of Corporation

* You can raise funds through the sale of shares in your business.

It is not your personal responsibility to be responsible for the debts that are you incur as a business.

* The business is taxed as an entity separate from the company and often has less tax.

* You may also keep the assets of your business in its name, not your own, so that they aren't the subject of lawsuits against

you personally. You may also deduct business expenses from your earnings.

* You may sell the assets of your business and then distribute the proceeds to yourself, and not pay tax.

The name of your company will be known to those who might be interested in doing business with you or purchase your services or products. In general, a corporate (or S-Corp) appears to be more reliable as well as "legit" than sole proprietorship.

The disadvantages of Corporation

A corporation's formation involves filing documents with either the state government or the federal government. It is expensive to incorporate and you'll have to pay tax upon the distribution of dividends.

* Additionally Certain taxes are payable in full, whereas personal taxes are only assessed on dividends.

* The net business earnings of the company is taxed twice - once at corporate rates and another time when the shareholder gets the dividends. These dividends are usually assessed at higher taxes.

* You must be ready for the meticulous records-keeping that is required for operating as a company. This is not only the business transactions you have to keep in the loop. This will also impact any personal transactions, which includes personal assets such as your car home, property and more.

* You can't return the property you transfer to your company.

* You are required to earn a salary which is taxed at your tax rate on income.

Small Corporation

A S Corporation is an entity that has the option of deciding the amount of profit it pays in dividends to shareholders and the amount that is paid as salary, which is assessed as personal tax. It is possible that the S Corp can also decide to not pay any profits to shareholders and instead keep the profits in its bank account and you'll need to invest your own money in the event that there's a shortage of funds.

The advantages of Small Corporation

* The net business earnings of the company is taxed only once.

* You pay less taxes (although this might not be necessary if you factor the salary payment).

* S Corps allow you to divide your earnings and dividends. This means you don't have to pay high taxes on all of it in one go. In this way, you could opt to collect your entire salary in one go and put off dividends for future dates.

* You are able to set up retirement accounts with an S Corp, meaning that you don't need undergo the exact process with an additional business entity when you intend to create another.

In contrast to ordinary companies, S Corps are not required to hold annual meetings , or take resolutions.

Advantages of S Corporation

* They're limited by the amount of shareholders they may possess, meaning that you are unable to offer shares to the general public - and you are able to issue up 100 shares. The only way is any person who is not employed by your business can be an investor.

* Salary payments can be a way to offset the savings by lowering the tax rate.

* Being taxed in the S Corp's income tax bracket means you'll have to pay taxes prior to when the tax rate if working as a solo proprietorship or general partnership, in which profits are taxed only when they are achieved by way of the distribution of dividends.

Limited Liability Company (LLC)

An LLC works like the corporation in the sense that it allows individuals to reduce self-employment tax and also retain assets under the company's name. It also has more flexibility than a company in regards to income distribution , and also avoids the double taxation (like S Corp). S Corp).

Benefits to Limited Liability Company (LLC)

* You may choose the method to tax your business by filing Form 8832 that determines the percentage of the profits generated by your LLC can be declared as personal tax.

* You are able to divide the profits of your business in any way you wish to. This could include taking salaries as dividends, taking

dividends and even distributions that are not even made.

Like normal corporations the LLC LLC doesn't have the obligation to have annual meetings or make resolutions.

* The LLC is not required to undergo an official probate procedure in the case of death.

Advantages from Limited Liability Company (LLC)

Your financial obligation is limited to the amount of the amount you invest in the company and you are not required to settle personal debts with company assets.

* The process of forming an LLC is more complicated than sole proprietorships or general partnership.

Self-Employment

If you decide to take the self-employment route, all taxes related to business will be included in your tax rate. In the event that you operate as a sole proprietorship or general partnership. In this situation, you are required to be taxed on all your earnings immediately after they have been realized (i.e. when the customer purchases the purchase of a product or service). For a company tax structure, taxes will be paid by corporate on its net earnings and after that, it is taxed when they are paid to shareholders as dividends from shareholders.

In the US self-employed earnings that exceeds $400 is tax-deductible. However, only when you report Schedule C. Also, there aren't any special credits or deductions that are available to self-employed people. In the UK, self-employment tax is tax exempt. UK also requires those who are self-employed to pay tax on their earnings when they have been realized. In Australia you can opt to be taxed by your income tax or by a separate taxation for business system. The EU has a common system of corporate taxation in which earnings from small-scale self-employed businesses is taxed under the personal earnings.

Benefits of Self-employment

* There are less forms to fill out for self-employed persons all through the year.

You are in complete control over the way you spend your earnings via dividends, salary, or any other distribution.

Dividends are taxed on less than your earnings if you worked as an employee.

* You are able to deduct the cost of expenses from your income as a business, which is a part of the tax-deductible amount total which will save you tax.

Advantages of Self-Employment

* You'll need to pay self-employment tax, which are often in the same range as regular tax rates on income.

Once you've reached the amount of $400 net income (called"tax floor"), or $400 in net earnings (also known as "tax ceiling") then you have to submit an Schedule SE with your IRS forms every year since the Revenue Code requires this Self-employment Tax to be as high as when you were employed.

* You might experience losses in your initial few years due to the initial financial investments.

* All profits earned are subject to Social Security and Medicare tax and income taxes

The rate is equal to 12.4 percent Social Security tax and a 2.9 Medicare tax on net earnings (totaling 15.3 percent).

If you are hiring employees, you'll have to take into consideration Federal Unemployment Tax Act (FUTA) taxes of 6.6% of the first $7000 paid to each employee each year, which will be used to fund the unemployment program run by the federal government.

There is no separation between personal and business assets.

General Partnership

General partnerships are the simplest and most affordable option to establish a company. It doesn't require formal filings with the government or any approval from agencies, like LLCs and corporations do. What is required is a verbal and/or written arrangement between two to three persons who wish to do business in partnership. The major benefit for this type of partnership is its ease in forming and dissolving it compared to other legal organizations. If there are disputes between the owners, things could become very complicated as there aren't rules for dividing the profits or assets fairly.

A general partnership has to pay taxes as part of the Partnership Taxation system, which means you'll be taxed on your net income only once per year. Profits are distributed according to the investment of each partner within the venture.

Benefits of General Partnership

* You can launch your business in a short time without having to worry about formalities such as the articles of incorporation and bylaws.

* If you're an owner of a small-sized business that doesn't require employees it is one of the most cost-effective and simple ways to begin.

You are able to dissolve the company without needing to file any documents or undergo an administrative process similar to what you would for other legal organizations.

Advantages of General Partnership

The tax on profits is personal earnings for both partners, meaning the tax rate you pay will be rather high (depending on the amount you earn).

It is not possible to create a distinction between the liabilities and assets of each partner.

* You are not able to sell your business without buying the share of the other partner, or locating a person who will become your new partner.

* If you don't enjoy how your business partner runs or invests their money You cannot quit the business without dissociating from your belongings and liquidating them.

Partnership of Professionals

Professional partnerships occur where two or more professional, such as accountants, physicians and lawyers come together to offer their services. Each partner is accountable for the self-employment tax they pay that are imposed in the exact same manner as individuals' income taxes. Professionals also need to submit the Schedule C with their tax form each year.

Benefits to Partnership of Professionals

* Professional partnerships do not require any documents and government authorization.

* In certain circumstances it could even result in an income tax deduction.

Advantages and disadvantages from Partnership of Professionals

* Each partner must have an accountant who can handle taxes that are double.

If you decide to end the partnership, it could be extremely costly and difficult due to how profits are distributed (i.e. in accordance with each participant's share in the partnership)

How to Select the Best Legal Organization for Your Business

When you're deciding on the best way to organize your small enterprise, it is important to think about the kind of expansion you'd like to see. For instance, if you're planning to expand your company and employ employees, you'll most likely need an LLC or a corporation instead of a sole proprietorship.

A general partnership or sole proprietorship is the ideal legal structure for your business when you are planning to run an ephemeral business and do not anticipate ever growing sufficiently to be able to hire employees. If your business is going to be managed by multiple individuals and involves complex decision-making processes Consider an LLC since it has more flexibility than general partnerships.

It is important to take into consideration a variety of aspects when you are deciding on the type or legal structure your small-scale business needs to be. The largest corporations possess the most facilities for hiring employees as well as managing complex issues however, they need a lot of documents and approval from the government. Smaller companies with few employees or plans for growth typically have fewer advantages to operating as a company. General partnerships are an option for small-sized businesses who don't want to take on the expense of establishing an official legal entity. However, it has the potential for risk and obligations.

It is recommended to think about your goals for the future prior to deciding on a legal structure. The most appropriate course of action will depend on the type of business you'd like start and the number of people who are involved in the running of it. There are pros and cons to every type of partnership. However, it's always recommended to consult with an attorney before making any decision, no regardless of the option you select. So, you can make sure that you are in a position to fulfill all your tax and legal obligations as the business owner.

Chapter 4: Startup Finances And Budgeting

One of the most important issues entrepreneurs must address is the financial management. The initial years of a business startup could be among the most challenging when you try to identify the right product or service that will bring in revenue, attract a desired quantity of customers, as well as price points that generate a steady income. This process is known as "bootstrapping."

There's only one chance at making it perfect. If you don't calculate your numbers correctly your business may not last for the next year. There are a variety of startup strategies with each having their pros and cons. There are few entrepreneurs who can afford to invest a large amount of money, or follow an idea that is unlikely to be profitable, however over-conservatism is also not a good idea.

Startups employ a variety of approaches to managing finances but generally are in one or more of the five areas in their financial management strategies. While you review this list, take note of the type of financial management approach your company will likely follow at the beginning of its development. Reading these tips can increase your understanding and knowledge of the best ways to manage your startup's financials.

A Financial Management Style of Successful Startups

1. Bootstrapping

Bootstrapping is the management approach used by the majority of entrepreneurs due to the fact that it requires minimal or no funds as well as allows a business to keep its ownership in full and result in a limited number of investors having a say in what happens to your business. This approach requires careful planning and a thorough knowledge of the expenses associated in the development of your product. It is also essential to be aware of any licensing requirements imposed by your state, local as well as federal governments.

If you choose to adopt a bootstrapping way of managing your finances you decide to follow, you'll be accountable for all costs until the point at which you are profitable. Although this is the case for the majority of startups, early-stage businesses that don't require external funding have to learn to live with what they can afford. In the end, the amount of imagination and innovation required from founders of startups is typically high.

2. Slow Growth

This method has been employed by numerous successful startups which have seen their growth steadily increase in the course of time, generating income by gradually gaining and retaining customers. In these conditions the company is able to be patient in deciding the amount of capital it will need to raise, the amount of revenue it'll require and when during its existence it should begin to approach investors.

The most important benefit of this method is that you have the control of your startup. But, since you're not making a lot of money initially most of the financial burden falls to the founders as well as early investors. Furthermore, investors may be wary of investing in a company that doesn't seem to be on a fast pace, particularly if the company seeks seed capital.

3. Rapid Growth

Many founders who are new should concentrate on establishing customers as fast as they can. However, successful companies often adhere to the opposite approach of investing in R&D (R&D) prior to investing in revenue generation.

The most important reason to adopt this method is that you will gain an edge over competitors that are in your sector when you're the first company to introduce a new service or product. However, as the majority of startups don't have enough funds to spend on R&D This is typically not the most efficient way to generate revenues.

4. Mix and match

In most cases it is a mixture of both strategies - also known as a hybrid strategy - is employed in cases where founders aren't sure how long they'll be in the beginning stage before they seek external funding. The business will invest in R&D and also build its client base through selling the products or services they plan to sell to generate income after the product is designed. This approach requires founders to balance the amount they invest and the speed at which they will spend it, while also generating enough revenue to sustain their own startup and to grow it.

5. Relying upon Friends and Family

This style of financial management lets you remain completely in control of your venture while allowing family members or friends members to pay for your expenses. The main drawback is that you'll not have the time to build your business since you'll be in charge of the day-today finances. If your donors are unable or unwilling pay for all your expenses it could be necessary to look for other funding sources in the near future.

Finance Options for Startups

There are several possible sources of financing that might be available to you when you're building your business. But, this list isn't exhaustive and is intended to serve as an introduction to study how much each one costs and the terms they provide.

1. Personal Savings

The money you've saved in the past is likely to be the most effective source of capital for your startup that allows you to keep the complete control of your business's direction and how it's operated. But, this might not be a viable choice for many entrepreneurs since many do not have enough funds to finance their ventures completely.

2. Personal Credit and Credit Cards and

Credit cards and loans can offer a start-up with low-interest, short-term finance. However, this type of financing typically has high interest rates. It is often difficult for startups to repay when they are not able to generate income rapidly. In addition, even although credit is simple to get, you'll be unable to find a lender with favorable conditions.

3. Crowdfunding

Crowdfunding is among the most well-known methods of funding startups in the present. The concept is that a lot of investors invest tiny amounts of money to help a company to finance its growth by transferring equity. It is nevertheless important to be aware that many startups do not meet their fund-raising goals , and they will not have anything to give in exchange. Furthermore, this process could take longer than anticipated and you could have to surrender some of the equity in your company.

4. Grants

Grants are usually offered by either the government or educational institutions, and require that startups satisfy certain criteria to be eligible for the grants. It is among the most popular options due to the fact that it offers startup founders the capital they need and requires a small equity stake in exchange. It is however very difficult to get an award of a grant. Your startup has to satisfy the criteria of every organisation you approach.

Making investments

It's crucial to recognize that a business doesn't require immediate, generalized success. Start by going to a specific market, and expand into other related markets once you have the money. If you're concerned about the location you'll receive the funds you require you don't need to worry. It is important to remember that all businesses must begin somewhere. In some situations, it's better to invest instead of waiting for the right moment.

There are two types of models for businesses such as brick-and-mortar, or home-based or online. Each type of business has its own cost of starting However, they are able to be managed with the budget low.

1. Brick-and-Mortar Businesses

This kind of business typically has a higher cost of starting because it requires the purchase of inventory, real estate and furniture. There are a variety of methods to cut down on these costs, for instance, leasing instead of buying real estate, or renting office space rather than leasing retail spaces. A broker's help to find the lowest rate for these costs is the most effective way to save money.

However, the expenses of furniture and inventory are usually considered to be permanent startup costs since they are required until the company can afford replacement. It is crucial to think about the time frame it will take your company to generate enough income to pay for these expenses when making purchases. Here are some expenses that are associated with these expenditures:

• Real estate fee: Lease, rent or purchase of property for commercial use, which includes the leasing of equipment.

* Cost of Inventory: The expenses that are incurred when purchasing inventory to sell within your business. It could include the materials used to create wholesale items to resell, and so on.

• Office Furniture cost related to purchasing furniture for your company such as chairs, desks tables, tables, as well as storage cabinets.

2. Home-based or online-based businesses

This kind of start-up is more affordable than brick-and-mortar businesses because it doesn't require the purchase of inventory or commercial real estate. But, you'll have to figure out the initial costs associated with setting up your company, creating your website and marketing.

* Startup Costs They are the costs that are associated with the start-up of a company that is not categorized into other categories like the creation of a logo or brand, establishing websites, creating flyers or business cards. They could include the

beginning advertising costs, or the purchase of items for the company.

* Operating expenses They are the expenses that are associated with running your home-based or online business on a regular basis, such as web design and hosting fees, and research costs that are related to the expansion of the range of your products or services. Examples of these costs include hosting costs for your website, and the expense of research materials when you're expanding into new markets.

* Additional Costs They are fixed expenses which will be paid each month to ensure that your business is functioning well and effectively. Examples include the deductibles (like insurance) and utility bills for the month like electricity and internet.

Calculating the Startup Costs

Calculating the cost of starting a business is a difficult process and should be inclusive of all costs related to the start of your company and your marketing plan. It is beneficial to create an inventory of all the expenses you anticipate incurring and then estimate the average cost for each. It is possible that certain expenses, like insurance premiums or legal costs depend on the service you buy and it is therefore important to determine an average cost for each type of.

In the beginning it is necessary to make investment for your business if you want to succeed and expand. They could be:

1. Product Development

A lot of startups have to put a lot of amount of time and money in creation of products as their ideas could not be viable or even profitable without thorough research and plan. If your business receives funds from a different source, such as grants. In this case you might not have to invest in these ventures in the beginning. But, it is crucial for your business to have an emergency cash reserve always and provide the required information to investors regarding the progress of their research and development efforts.

2. Marketing and Advertising

These two are the most important elements of any business that is successful as they enable the business to present their products or services to customers and influence their purchases. But, this kind of expenditure is not necessary for every startup, particularly those that operate in a well-established sector in which their product or service is likely to draw customers.

3. Operating expenses

Every startup must cover its operating expenses day-to day in order to be successful. They can be anything that includes paying workers to leasing office space. However, the cash the startup earns through sales will pay for the majority of these costs and leave you with a minimum of extra ongoing expenses, unless your business grows substantially in the course of time.

4. Inventory

Another significant cost for startup companies is the cost of inventory. If the startup sells an item, it has to have sufficient inventory available in all times to provide for its clients. But if the company only provides services there aren't any extra costs that come with this kind of expenditure.

5. Other startup costs

There are numerous expenses to prepare for when you start an enterprise including incorporation fees licensing and permits, consulting services, as well as office equipment. Depending on the industry you are in as well as your location costs could amount to tens of thousand of dollars, or greater. If you manage your budget well and make wise spending decisions you will be able to cover all your startup expenses in a matter of 6 months, or even less.

You can evaluate your average expenses for starting up with your expected revenues to figure out how long it will take for your business to turn a profit. Once you've determined the estimated profitability margin (your annual earnings minus expenses) by multiplying that figure by 12 will provide you with an estimate of the time it will be to make to a profit. For instance that your expected annual earnings are $100,000, and your monthly average expenses are around $8000, your expected profit margin will be $12,000. Then, multiplying that by 12 gives we an estimation of the amount of months required before your business is profitable.

To make the initial costs easier to manage If you want to make your startup costs more manageable, set an amount of your earnings each month in order to reduce the burden of the amount of debt. Consider, for instance, that your monthly loan payments are $500. You can put aside 10 percent of your income towards this monthly installment. In that scenario, this will shorten the time needed for the debt to be paid back in one calendar year.

The Loan Payments, Interest Rates and Personal Assets

The amount of time it will take your business to reach profitability is a crucial aspect of the process of starting a new business. But, there are additional factors to keep in mind when you are determining the amount you'll require to borrow to begin your venture, which includes what amount of interest that you have to pay for the loan.

If you're borrowing a loan for business the lender must supply specific details regarding any conditions pertaining to the loan in written form. This includes the duration and repayment terms as well as any percentage rates that apply to missed or late installments. It is possible to use this information to figure out the amount you'll be required to budget in order for the repayment term. If you are able make it, it's a good idea to pay for bigger installments in your first stages of your company to pay down the principal balance of your loan as soon as is possible.

Additionally, be aware that certain personal assets like your home or car such as your home, for example, cannot be used to pay business debt. If however, the lender could prove that your company has failed due to negligence or negligence, then they might be able confiscate any personal assets that are not essential to the business that you have.

When you start a new business, you'll be required to plan your initial expenses to minimize debt and stop the bank from tightening its purse strings. There are numerous ways that you can cut back on ongoing expenses while maintaining a steady flow of customers by finding a cheap space for your business or holding pop-up sales at special occasions.

Be aware of the costs and rate you'll need be paying for the business will aid you in determining whether borrowing the best option. If yes, carefully making your budget in accordance with the specifics of your loan contract will help you to adhere to the deadline for repayment and be back on track planning for the purchase of the purchase of new inventory or equipment.

Chapter 5: Writing Your Business Plan

The writing of a business plan is, simply put the most important action you can take to ensure success. In the absence of a plan, your venture is just an idea. You'll have something to compare against a business plan when you begin your business. This chapter gives a brief overview of a business's plan and the reason why you must prepare one if you're launching your own business. It also walks you through the process of creating a business plan.

What is the reason to write a business plan?

If you're planning to launch an enterprise, you may already realize that having an effective business plan is crucial. Simply put, your business plan will help to define your business by jotting down all you be aware of in one spot. It's also a way to gauge your progress against. Writing the right plan will aid you in achieving your goals for the business. The business plan could serve as a guideline to write an official business plan to give to investors and bankers, partners or any other.

Additionally to that, writing a business strategy can help you remember crucial specifics. For instance, if you're selling a product the plan should outline your market of choice and the methods you'll use to reach them. If you're starting an enterprise that is based on services and you're looking to expand into other areas over the course of time. If that's the situation the business plan you write should be a discussion of strategies for growth. Also creating a business plan can help you keep all of your research into your business accessible in one location.

What Should It Contain?

Your business plan should contain the answers to these questions: What's the goals for your company? What amount of money do you require to start and how do you raise that amount? What are your competitions? What is their position on the market? What is the best way to present your company? What is the current market and how much do you think you could take advantage of? What can you do to convince customers to purchase the products you're offering? These are only a few aspects you'll have to consider.

The business plan you write may contain several sections, based on your objectives and how many details you'd like to include. If, for instance, you're preparing a business plan to obtain a loan or ask an investor to provide capital, it's most likely that your business plan will include these sections

Executive Summary Executive Summary: An executive summary is an overview of your business plan, designed to draw the attention of potential customers. It provides the motivation behind your company and the goals you're hoping to achieve. It is recommended that the executive summary not exceed one page.

The Company Description section will describe your company or organisation, including the mission statement as well as the services you intend to provide. This could be the only official section that you have in your company plan and if you're looking for financial assistance or any other type of support this is the ideal time to talk about the amount of money you're seeking and the reasons you're seeking it.

Market Analysis This section can assist readers to understand what customers might want or require what the size of there is a market for your goods or services, and also where your competitors are located in the market. If you could stack your competitors over each other What would they look like to you? What will you do to differentiate yourself from your competition?

The Company's Strategy is the time when you talk about your team with regard to its strengths and weaknesses as well as how the business plan will assist you in reaching your objectives. If you're seeking potential investors, partners or even shareholders now is the best time to outline your exit strategies, which might be appealing to them.

The Management Team section will be a description of the roles your team has and obligations, as well as members' abilities and their qualifications.

Financial Projections/Pro-Formas: If you're looking for funding, now is when you'll want to share your financial plan in the form of pro formas or financial projections. These can be created using free templates that can be found on the internet.

Marketing Strategy: If you're trying to bring customers into your business, this section will define the steps you can take to accomplish this target.

Action Plan Action Plan: This is the place to outline the steps you must take to accomplish your goals including specific deadlines for each job. The final step should be the list of actions items or tasks you must accomplish.

How Long Should It Last?

A typical business plan can range between 20 and 100 pages. Although it can be written in handwriting or written using computers, it's easier to write these documents in the format of a Word as well as a Google Docs document. If you're writing a company plan that you will only use for yourself it's fine to add only those sections that you'll need. If you're in search of financial assistance or any other type of support it is recommended to present the entire plan including all of its parts in order would be beneficial. At the end of the day your business plan should be comprehensive and complete.

When is it best to finish?

Many experts suggest creating a business plan no after you're able in presenting it to prospective shareholders or investors. However, writing a plan might be too early when your company is still in its beginning stages and is still in the development stage. It's fine to begin with a brief description of your business and leave out analyses of the market, financial forecasts as well as other formal areas. One of the most crucial things is to create your plan for business as quickly as you can, so you're able to benefit from the process of planning within the process.

How Do I Start?

The first step is to determine the objective for your plan. If you're looking for financial or other forms of assistance, it's essential to include all the elements of the formal business plan. If you're writing your own business plan solely for your own use you should only include the parts that you think are the most pertinent. Be aware that the more thorough and complete your plan, the more prepared you'll be when you begin on a venture.

Here is an example outline of the business plans you have in mind. Be aware the outline below is intended for the complete business plan. If you're creating a business plan to be used only for personal use remove those sections that aren't relevant to you or your company. It's broken down into five major sections that most entrepreneurs have in their plans: executive summaries market analysis, a the company's plan, strategy for management and an action plan. Take this information as a reference when you write your business's plan.

1. Executive Summary

The executive summary is the very first section in your plan for business. It's usually a two- or one-page summary of your overall plan, and should be a clear description of your company's strategy and provide a summary of the financial forecasts. This is where you should include the following details:

• A description of your business as well as the purpose of your business

* The nature the business plans you have

* Each of the sections in the plan of business

* Name of the company and motive for the establishment of the company.

* Mission statement

• Descriptions of the product or services (including the patents related to them)

* Focus on the market and the customer

* Goals and goals and

The financial projections must be included, which include the income statement for at minimum three years, if feasible. If you don't have sufficient information to create a complete financial forecast just include a complete one-year budget.

2. Market Analysis

Market analysis is the process where you discuss the current situation of your industry , and also provide specifics about your competitors with respect to their strategies and strategies. This section can help you determine whether there's a space on the market to your business and how large this potential market could be, and the names of your competitors. It is also important to note any trends emerging which could impact your business or your industry. The section on your business plan should include the people who are your customers and what their requirements are. It is important to include details regarding the size of the market, the trends in the business and ways to satisfy the needs of customers better than what your competitors are doing.

Include the following details:

* A brief introduction that explains the intent behind this section

Market segmentation as well as trends within your field

* Analysis of competitor's strategies and tactics

* A brief description of the business and its rate of growth

The position of your company in your field, including SWOT analysis (Strengths and weaknesses, opportunities and Threats)

* How many rivals do you have? what do they are up to

* Your primary competencies

* The strengths of the management team including biographies for the most important staff members

3. Company Strategy

This section explains how you can satisfy the demands of the market better than your competitors. It also outlines the strengths and weaknesses of your business. The section should also outline your company's role in the market and include any specialization or niche you intend to utilize to make a unique selling point. This section should cover every aspect of your company, including the product range and the channels for sales, marketing, and promotions strategies, pricing and value proposition manufacturing processes and capabilities, the location of production facilities, as well as logistics to bring your product or service to the market. It should also contain the copy of your business plan as the foundation on the basis of your operation, along with pricing and costs. Additionally, you must include the following details:

An introduction that explains the reason for this section

Your firm's position on market and competitors

• Your business's strengths as well as strengths and

* The mission of the company and its the core principles (used to make decisions, including those relating to marketing)

• Market position: Who will purchase your product or service and what type and type of service offer to them

The key strategies are marketing strategies as well as key marketing techniques for implementing those strategies

* A summary of the services and products

* Competitive advantage - how do you will win new customers as well as keep those you already have

4. The Management Team as well as the Action Plan

In the section on management teams within your company plan you'll need to provide a concise description of each member in your leadership team with their professional qualifications, which include qualifications, certificates or licenses, as well as memberships in relevant associations related to industry. Include their roles within your business to help you determine the guidelines to run your company.

Use this procedure for each manager team member:

1. Write a brief explanation of what they do and what they do in the business.

2. Provide their credentials and their experiences.

3. Include their contact details (include the contact details to provide references).

4. Write down each team member's key accomplishments, including the specific outcomes they have achieved which are relevant to their current work.

5. Give a brief explanation of what you'd like the person to accomplish in the first year of their position (e.g. the number of products that are developed for new markets and the percentage of sales that result from the new marketing techniques, etc.).

6. Define how you will track the progress of your product (e.g. for example, reporting on a monthly basis on new products).

7. Define your plans for succession to every important post if needed.

Your business plan for your business should contain an outline of your company and all important activities that need to be accomplished to meet your objectives. The plan should be realistic and precise, with each task divided into a schedule to complete.

5. Financial Plan

Your financial plan forms the basis of your business's overall plan. It should include precise information on the methods you plan to use to create cash flow and income and provide supporting data which outlines your expectations and goals, such as:

Price of Product: List the itemized costs and suggested prices per unit for each item or service. Include price adjustments throughout the duration of the company and, if needed. If you are planning to market a portion of your goods at less than the list price, you must explain that, and explain how your company will compensate for the price difference.

* Operating expenses Include the total month-long operating costs (salaries rent, utilities as well as travel costs and more.)

* Capital Costs: Equipment acquisitions and other major purchases required to start your business (e.g. land or building for a distribution centre). In the notes, you should specify how you anticipate these purchases to be paid for.

* Estimated revenue is based on your plans for each quarter of the beginning year, and for the whole year, which includes projections of expansion (or decline) between years 2 and 5 (based on assumptions in your business model).

* A thorough description of your financial plan including:

a. Sources of funding for companies (what is the purpose of the funding and to fund what)

b. A complete cash flow forecast that lists the sources of income as well as expenses each month for the beginning of the year.

a. Forecasts for years 2-5 If available

b. Projection of financial statements (income statement balance sheet, income statement, and statements of cash flows)

Include a roadmap of how you plan for your company to grow in the course of five years.

* Projections should be broken up into quarters, indicating how you intend to sustain the initial successes.

If you're contacting potential investors for funding you, be sure to include this information (for instance, what percentage of equity you're willing to surrender).

6. Appendix

The appendix provides sources that offer more details regarding your business or details on the subject. This includes:

* Financial statements for companies, such as balance sheet income statement and cash flow statement

* Business plan elements such as operations, marketing and profiles of management teams

* Prototype models of the products or services you plan to market

Referral list (include references to back your credentials)

Copy of legal papers, such as contracts between clients and vendors leases, patents

Other Important Information

Include a table contents and an executive overview (a short overview of the most important elements that you want to include in your company plan).

* For certain businesses there may be a need to incorporate risk analysis and mitigation strategies. For other businesses, you may be able to include an inventory of possible challenges and the way you plan to deal with these.

* If you're looking for investors, give the ways they could expect to earn a profit for their money.

* Use graphs and charts to demonstrate your strategy using numbers, percentages or other units that are measurable. They should be simple to read and comprehend.

* The style of writing must be professional and free of mistakes in spelling or mistakes. It is recommended to get at minimum one person to review your business plan.

* The length of the document is contingent on how extensive you'd like it to make it. If the reader is only looking for an overview of your business, keep your message short and concise. You can go into greater detail when they request more information or are seeking investors.

The plan you choose to use should have an elegant appearance So, get someone to assist with the formatting and visual aids.

The process of writing your business plan can be laborious, but it's also an the chance to demonstrate the amount of effort and thought has gone into the business. There's every time more than one method of accomplishing a new business concept and there is more than one solution to the issue in present. The key to creating your company plan is to demonstrate the way you've researched your idea and then come up with an effective strategy that is feasible. The purpose of your strategy for business is to show investors and lenders that your plan will be successful on the ground, therefore it is essential to prove you've conducted your own research. It is possible to use information that come from research on market conditions or previous experience to prove you're well-versed in the field and the requirements to be successful.

Chapter 6: The Branding Strategy Strategies

And Identity

It is the science and art of invoking an emotion in customers that they connect with both value and image to a service, product or company. The impression isn't physical. It's all in the customers' mind and is affected through a variety of factors like the price and design and physical location, salespeople and even media. So, branding is not an event that happens once. It requires constant reevaluation and adaptation to the present context because external factors are constantly changing.

Advertising is different from branding. Branding is a broad strategy, whereas advertisements are a particular activity that is used to enhance the image of a brand. Advertising is typically considered to be something you watch on television or listen to on the radio or read in magazines or newspaper. Many people make use of the terms branding and advertising interchangeably however they're distinct in their fundamental.

84

Branding is not the design of a logo or color choice though they are both part of the method. Branding is a strategy and an identity. It begins with knowing the direction you want your company to be, and then is completed when customers associate particular feelings with the products and services that you offer. In this section we will concentrate on the process of creating and managing the branding of your company. We will also discuss methods and tricks to guide the development of your brand's strategy and design.

Brand Strategy

Plan, or Brand Strategy It is among the most essential branding components. It defines the entirety of your brand, such as your target audience and competitors, voice, goals, niche markets guidelines for style, and the tone of voice. The strategy for your brand should be created along with an overall business plan that includes useful content to the document describing the strategy. It's more than the products or services. Branding is the depiction of a company's image and should be a reflection of your service or product offering as well as your company's values and values.

The strategy for branding will define how you would like to appear in the eyes of your customers as well as your intended audience. It encompasses the overall image of the business as well as specific messages that you wish to communicate. Your strategy for branding must be a reflection of your values and mission as a company. It's not just about items or services. Branding is the depiction of a business's image and should include the product or service that you provide as well as your business's values and culture.

A brand's strategy must be reviewed annually in order to assess any changes to the external environment that can impact your competitive advantage. The company's values must remain in line with the consumer's needs and desires for this strategy to function efficiently.

How to Create an effective Brand Strategy

Step One: Get to know your target market and be aware of your brand. Determine the kind of customer you wish to reach with clear demographics.

Step Two: Determine the brand's essence. Simply put, it is the essence that is what makes a business distinctive and distinct from rivals in the market.

Step 3: Design your brand's strategy. The brand strategy outlines precisely how you intend to reach out to your public and keep the promises you made in the second step.

Step Four The fourth step is to write an outline of the style guidelines for your logo's colors, color scheme, text as well as other. A style guide guarantees the marketing material created for your company will be in sync and reflect your brand's values and the principles.

Step Five: Create a pop culture-friendly tagline to be included in your brand's logo, style guides and. The tagline must convey the essence of what you do but should be brief enough that people can remember.

The company's brand strategy can affect how the public sees them and also how they are perceived by competitors. When creating a new branding strategy, you must think about and incorporate all your company's communication tools in the process of creating it, such as marketing, advertising materials such as letterheads, business cards, and billboards. Effective branding requires that each communication tool in the same way to convey your message in the exact same way to clients.

Strategies for Implementing an effective brand Strategy

• Be clear and concise Write down the advantages of your service or product and the things that differentiate you from your competitors.

Have A Voice Make use of adjectives to explain the experience customers will have when making use of your products and services. For instance, if your brand is lively young, energetic and vibrant and energetic, that should be evident through the branding.

* Utilize Benchmarking: Know the direction you'd like to take and develop your strategy in line with. Plan out a strategy and be aware of the strategies of your competition so that you can stand above the rest.

• Be consistent: all marketing tools like business cards, signage lettersheads, billboards, and letterheads must perform in harmony and align with the overall strategy of branding.

* Remain Memorable The most popular brands worldwide are distinguished by their unique brand identity that is easily communicated via their branding strategy.

Do not forget to review your branding strategy on a regular basis Take note of how your company as well as your competition and market has changed over time, and adjust in line with the changing environment. Be aware that your branding strategies should represent your organization's fundamental values. It's vital to stay conscious of the way customers see these values.

The branding Strategy can affect the success of a business

A well-designed branding strategy could result in increased sales, a higher level of customer loyalty and also possibilities for partnerships with other businesses in similar markets. People are more likely to buy from a brand they are connected to and have confidence in. If you can make your customers feel certain things by applying your brand strategy, they are more likely to return.

A well-planned brand strategy will ensure that every aspect of your advertisements work in the same way. For instance, suppose that your website is using one color scheme while your billboards have a different. In this scenario there could be an inconsistency between what users can see on the internet and what they see in print. To prevent this from happening ensure that the colours, layout and even the words represent your branding strategy.

A well-constructed branding strategy will communicate your business's values to prospective customers. In creating an image that you are proud of through your branding strategy you will ensure that your customers remember the way your company's products or services affect them. If they are able to relate to your business in this way then you're more likely to win their trust over your competition.

It is essential to consider the overall branding strategy in the creation of marketing materials for an upcoming product or service. With a thorough understanding of branding strategies it will be possible to effectively communicate your company's image and mission effectively to your customers.

Brand Identity

Brand identity is undoubtedly among the top crucial aspects of marketing. It is commonly called "the visuals" as it is concerned with the way your business presents itself by using things like your logo or fonts, as well as your website style. The brand identity is the appearance and feel of your company's communications tools. It also covers typesetters, color schemes and designs for business cards and other marketing tools. When you are developing a new branding strategy, it is important to take into consideration what your brand's image will look like. This involves looking at fonts, colors and the overall layout that your web site has. If everything is together it will be possible to convey your brand's message more effectively to potential clients.

Brand Identity Visual Components

* The Company Logo It is the image which represents your whole business. It should reflect the things your company is doing and

who you're trying to reach out to in all times.

• Business cards: It's crucial to make a strong first impression. A business card can be a great opportunity to showcase your brand's identity. Make sure that your business card looks professional, has the right fonts and colors and is accompanied by clearly stated call-to-action.

* Letterheads: Letterheads must be contemporary, informative and appealing. A modern font is a fantastic way to demonstrate that you're current.

• Envelopes: Your color as well as the logo and the design of your envelopes need to be consistent with the overall branding. If your envelopes are distinct from other envelopes that have been made, it could result in a disconnect between the messages that the consumer receives.

• Websites: A site isn't just about content, it's also a crucial symbol of your brand's image. With a professional-looking website that is clear in its images and hues, people are more likely to believe the legitimacy of your business.

Brand Identity - How to Make It Work

Once you've decided on the mission of your business and what you'd like to accomplish, you need to think about what you'll use to communicate the message. If your company is large or small the visual image that is effective in promoting your brand's image will produce the same impact. If you have a well-established brand image such as Coke or Google and you're not sure if it's beneficial to make a change.

Use your brand's image to attract a specific segment or market. For instance, if, for example, you're a funeral service and you want to attract more customers from younger people changing the colours and the fonts on your business cards could assist you in reaching your objectives. If you're feeling that your current branding isn't performing in the way you would like it to, experiment with a few ideas.

Attracting attention is among the primary goals when marketing your company. Because most businesses have similar characteristics, you'll be in competition with other businesses for clients. Therefore, if your company's current brand image isn't working, it's the time to make a change. Here are some simple ways to enhance your brand's image:

1. Change the color.

2. Modify the fonts and typography.

3. Edit or delete images.

4. Alter the design of your website or marketing materials. You can also change the layout of your the business card.

5. Bring in a new logo design.

When creating a brand new identity, you must be aware of what you're trying accomplish. This is where your plan begins. Once you've established the look and feel of your brand and what it is, you must decide how you will promote it , and to whom it will be targeted to.

After you've developed a new brand image for your company ensure that your customers notice by earning their confidence. If they are noticing your logo or website or business card is different, they're more likely look at it again. Be sure that these changes are consistent and reinforce the message of your brand. If you've accomplished this you'll be on right path.

Strategies for Creating a an Effective brand identity

While you may make use of your logo for an emblem of your company It's crucial to keep in mind that the visual representation of your brand helps people know the person you are and what you're about. Be sure that these three points are addressed prior to making any changesto your logo:

1. What's the background story of your business?

2. What do you think your company stands for?

3. What are you hoping to achieve with your brand's identity?

When you have which answer you need to know then you'll be able discover a visual representation of the process that is effective. If the design isn't working or requires some tweaking There are plenty of things that could be adjusted and altered before you get started. Here are a few of the most frequent issues that arise in branding for companies and the best way to prevent these issues:

1. Lack of a clear Purpose Lack of a clear purpose: A major issue in small companies is a absence of a strong brand name. With a clear mission statement, you can give your company the direction it requires to succeed and expand.

2. Overly generic: If your branding is plain or boring, people may think there's nothing important to say. If you keep an eye on the current trends in your industry and ensuring you stand out , but not too much like a copycat.

3. Not up to date If your brand's image is outdated or doesn't work to meet your goals The best solution is to create a new design and layout so that your customers are aware of what they can be expecting.

4. Too complex The logo may appear simple, but its branding must be consistent. If you make your site appear different from your flyers, business cards and other marketing materials your customers could be confused as to the message you're trying to convey.

5. There are no standards: It may seem more convenient to have several designs and colors, however, it's crucial to establish guidelines to ensure that everything

appears professional. This includes having consistent typography, having a distinct color scheme, and adhering to the standards that are essential to good graphic design.

6. It's Not in Harmony with Your Competitors Your Product or Idea isn't Unique: You may have a unique business concept or product however if it doesn't distinguish itself from the rest of the competitors it's at risk of not earning any money. If you keep your eye on trends in your field and observing the trends in your industry, you can ensure you're in the right place of originality and creativity.

7. The old brand identity may work for a while , but you need to be expanding and retaining the needs of customers to ensure an underlying consistency in your business's branding. It requires time and money but having a strong brand image will aid in retention of customers and help to make sense of your brand's identity and expansion.

8. Over-extended: It could be tempting to display all the things you're working on

however, if your brand becomes too cluttered, it's going create confusion for your customers. Determine the most important factors to be focused on in your strategy, then apply it as a foundation for your brand's identity prior to proceeding to other elements.

Brand Book

The template for a brand book was created to help standardize the communications of a brand. It covers everything from the elements that constitutes a brand's brand branding and management by introducing the fundamentals of design and application, up to the particulars of typography and colors. This gives business owners to examine all aspects of branding one place , so they can be assured that they're getting what require while reducing time and expense.

A branding book can be used to provide a manual for new employees as well as an easy reference to refer back to later. It's a chance for different individuals to gain an understanding of branding and the way it functions to ensure that everyone is working in enhancing and growing your brand's image. Everything you know about your brand is all in one place to all those who work with it to look at.

The brand book contains:

The fundamental elements of your brand's identity and the way they've been applied

The documentation of your reasoning behind your brand's identity including typography, colors, choices, and much more.

The logo's usage guidelines that covers everything from how to apply the logo and how to adjust it to the appropriate colors and fonts

Color palette guides will show the hex codes of each color you use within your company

* Use samples of your company's logo on diverse media, including print and digital media

Branding is an integral aspect of growing your business. It's about the style and appearance that attract or dissuade potential customers in a matter of seconds. It's therefore crucial to do it right to reach the people that you're trying to reach. The process of branding doesn't need to be a lengthy process, but you should be performing something since fashions and tastes change with time. The only method to keep your brand current is to dedicate yourself to it. This starts with a solid business image starting from the beginning, and continuing it throughout the years to come.

Chapter 7: Setting Up An Online Website

You've decided to start your own business. You have an idea you're interested in and wish to make money out of. A site for your small business will help you establish credibility online and shows that you're willing to invest into your business and consider your business as a viable venture. It's the most affordable method of marketing to potential customers even if it's the basic brochure website. You can create a free site with hosting, or opt for a premium plan which gives you more features and more control over the layout.

Small business websites are an essential element of building your brand. Your website is considered to be an extension of the business which allows you to communicate directly with new customers in the most efficient manner. This section will walk you through the process of creating a small-sized business website that is functional and cost-effective.

Guidelines for Creating the Website

1. Define the Purpose of Your Website

Before you begin signing up for hosting on the web make sure you know what your website is going to be employed to serve. It sounds easy but it's difficult to determine due to the many things that an organization could make use of the website to serve. Consider what you would like your website to accomplish for your small-scale company. You may have a number of purposes in your the back of your mind, but it's better to concentrate on one. It's simpler to promote the advantages of a specific reason.

When you've identified a goal then think about how this goal can be achieved. It is important to determine what kind of website would best suit your needs, and who will be using it, as well as how frequently. These questions will assist you to develop a great web site.

2. Select Your Platform

After you have decided on the goals of your website it is time to decide on the best platform. This involves deciding on what your site's design and function. Numerous platforms are accessible, ranging from free, open-source software to paid services offering numerous options. You must consider which one is the easiest to use for your needs and the amount of time you are willing to spend on its use, and if it can meet all the objectives your company requires through the website.

3. Select Your Design

Before you design websites, it's essential to determine the message you wish to communicate. There are a lot of free templates, but you may need to shell out extra money for custom services if you're looking for something that truly reflect the image of your business. Consider the reason you are designing a website and what you intend to achieve by it. This will help you make your choices for design more specific and assist you in choosing the most appropriate option to meet your needs.

4. Get Web Hosting

When you have your objectives as well as your platform and design choices set then the second step will be to find an hosting service. This must be properly set up before any actual coding work can begin. Determine how you wish to utilize your website and the type of traffic you're hoping to attract before you decide which hosting option is best for your website.

5. Register Your Domain Name

If you've got an account with a hosting provider and you've made a decision, you need to select your domain name. Domain names are the primary address of your website's address on the internet, therefore it must reflect the business's activities in the best way you can. It's best to keep it as brief as you can and easy to write as it is likely to be used frequently. Domain names are not associated with your hosting provider, so you can purchase it from a domain name service as well as host it your own. Also, you should consider whether you would like to utilize specific extensions that could make your website more visible on search results.

6. Designing Your Website

Now is the time to get into the details of creating your website. It can be accomplished using an interface that allows drag and drop or a website builder or even programming your website. Take a look at the platform you choose to use and your design preferences and how they impact the ease of building your website. None of these options are difficult, however you'll have to master the fundamentals of HTML If you're programming yourself. Consider how long it will take you to complete the task and also how patient then choose the option that is suitable for your needs.

7. Get Your Website Prepared for Publication

When your website is finished and you're happy with the outcome, it's now time to make it available. This is when you have to publish your website to allow people to locate your site by typing in the domain name into the search bar in their browser. It is possible to create your own website, however you can also sign up to an organization that provides publishing services. Take a look at your options, and then choose an easy one that can help your business to meet its objectives.

The Top Free Website Builders

After you've created your website, selected an appropriate platform, and mastered HTML If you need to now is the time to construct the website it self. This isn't a complex procedure, and you could employ a variety of tools based on the features you require. Take into consideration what your website requires and the possible traffic volume it could receive before choosing the best platform for your website.

1. Free Open-Source Software

WordPress is among the top well-known open-source, free platform and offers lots of features for websites that are growing. It allows you to design a website completely from scratch. There is a wide selection of widgets, themes and extensions to aid you in reaching your goals. yourself. Free versions are limited in the amount of pages that you can eliminate and certain features aren't available, however it's still an excellent start. It's completely free to set the foundation of a WordPress website. To make the most of the platform, you'll have to pay for hosting and buy more themes, plug-ins and widgets. If you're looking for the user-friendliness, an open-source platform that is free could be the right choice for you.

2. Builder Software for free on the Internet. Builder Software

If you don't need anything complicated and prefer to choose from a range of pre-designed templates, a no-cost website builder may be the right alternative for you. The software functions like Microsoft Word and is very easy to get. Although there are restrictions on what you are able to do, free site builders permit you to build an attractive and professional website in a matter of minutes.

The software that is described above is available for free and there are many themes to choose from, so this feature is not expensive. However, certain (or all) options may be limited according to the website builder you choose to use. If you're looking to reduce costs, this could be the right choice.

3. Pre-designed templates

If you'd prefer to use an already-designed template that you can modify the colors, images, and even the text to match your company, a site builder is a good option. They have a lot of templates. It's easy to locate one that fits your business brand's style and design. These platforms provide an easy drag and drop interface, which transforms into HTML code after you've published it.

The platform is free to use. There are restrictions in what you can create with the templates. There is the possibility of having to pay for additional customizable options. If you're looking to reduce costs and time, this could be the best choice.

4. Sites Dedicated to You

If your company requires high-tech technology, your best choice is to hire an expert designer to design your site for you. Designers charge a fee in exchange for their services however it's an investment into the growth of your company which will certainly yield dividends. You'll receive something distinctive that matches the exact style of your business's brand. This means that you will have a lot more control over your website, and you can rest assured that it is professional-looking. If your goal is to have complete control over your website's style, then hiring a professional is the best choice.

WordPress Vs. Web Builders for Free

If you're looking to reduce time and money It might be a good idea to choose a free website builder. These platforms are easy and simple to use which means you can design your website yourself and not pay any amount. However, if the capabilities of WordPress is a great choice for what you require It could be better to select this type of platform. It's completely free and easy to use, however it offers more options than a simple website builder.

If you prefer to select among a range from templates available, it may be worth considering templates-based or free website builders platforms. It allows you to build an appealing and professional website without having to spend any cash. If you're looking for complete control over your website and aren't afraid to pay an artist, hiring a designer to create your website for you might be the best choice.

Selecting a platform will be contingent on the requirements of your company. If you're trying to cut costs web-based builders that are free or templates-based platforms could be the right choice for you. If you'd prefer more control over your website's design and aren't afraid of having to pay for it, hiring an expert to design your site for you might be the best choice.

For companies that wish to sell their products, acquiring an Shopify website is the ideal choice. The platform can help you create quickly and effortlessly an online marketplace. It also offers a wide range of options that allow customers to buy items they need. If, however, you'd prefer to have a site focused on products, a personal site could be the best choice.

If you're looking in making it simple as it is for your customers to purchase from you and buy from you, then Shopify is the ideal option. It makes it extremely easy for customers to locate what they want. The platform also has features like live chat, in which they are able to contact you should they have any queries.

The Most Important Parts of an online site

If you want your website to succeed and draw the maximum number of customers the site must have an attractive image. It will be necessary to include certain elements like:

1. Logo

A well-designed logo can make your company appear more professional and well-established. It can also help clients to find you online when a colleague or friend has suggested them. However, how you choose to design your logo can vary from business-to-business. There aren't any hard and strict rules regarding this element however, you should select one that is consistent with your company's brand.

2. About Page

A profile page can help prospective buyers find out who they're purchasing from and what services the company provides. It's a good idea to provide information such as the length of time your company has been in operation as well as any awards or other recognition you've received, as well as the products you offer. This provides your customers with an idea of what they can expect when working with you. It also will help build trust between you and them.

3. Landing Page/Product Page

This is a vital aspect when selling services or products. If you wish customers to purchase from you, your website needs to be simple to locate the information they require. A landing page should include all the essential details regarding your product or service , and will provide a sense of what it's like working with you. The more professional the page appears the more likely it is that people will purchase from you.

4. Shopping Carts

This is an essential aspect of websites which sell services or products. If visitors can't find shopping cart buttons, they may not be aware that you provide this kind of service. More prominent the aspects are in your website, the more likely it is that customers are to purchase from your site. If they are looking for items on your site or other websites, doing it within a couple of clicks is crucial to increase the number of sales.

5. Contact Us/Help Section

If someone wants to know more about your business, or contact you with reasons of any kind, then it is a must on your website. If you provide customer service and customer support, it's essential that your contact information be readily accessible to ensure that customers can communicate promptly and effectively in case of any issues.

The most essential elements of a site are the most crucial elements that must be included in order for your website to function properly and be successful. If you want your site to appear professional it is vital to incorporate these elements on the website. It's also beneficial to include other elements like information pages about yourself, contacts details or shopping carts. This will allow your website to succeed and you'll witness an increase in number of people using it.

Chapter 8: Setting Up Social Media

If you are a small-scale business manager or owner it is essential to be on major social media platforms to get your brand name visible to clients. However, before you begin there are a few aspects to think about. What number of accounts will you require? What platforms should you choose? What kinds of images and videos are best for each platform? This chapter provides a summary of all the options for social media in order to help you understand how to setup your business's social media profiles efficiently. It also offers suggestions for using each platform to ensure your business can reap the greatest outcomes.

There are numerous social media websites available. Small businesses are likely to make use of Facebook, Instagram, LinkedIn, Twitter, TikTok, and YouTube. You might also want to consider adding a few more popular social networks based on your customer's demographics. Here's a list of the most popular social media platforms along with some benefits and drawbacks to companies:

1. Facebook

The year 2021 is when Facebook is expected to have 2.77 million monthly active users. That's that's more than half of the internet's users. Facebook is also becoming increasingly significant for companies that sell online since it's one of the most used platforms to post the pages of their products. The majority of young adults and millennials utilize this platform, with the focus being more on females. These groups comprise an overwhelming portion of small businesses targeted audiences.

Users make use of Facebook to stay in touch with family and friends and to keep track of what's happening in all the news around them and also share what they are interested in with their friends. However, this isn't the only reason why marketers utilize Facebook. People are using it to discover interesting products that they're interested in as well as to look up different brands' profiles on their network. It's something your business can make use of by boosting the presence of your company on Facebook.

Pros:

* Excellent for marketing on e-commerce since people are more likely to share the pages of their products

* Great for B2C marketing since consumers use it to discover interesting new products and services.

The advertising capabilities of Facebook make easy to display ads on the platform.

Excellent to provide customer support, branding recognition and lead generation

It allows you to target your customers based on their demographics, interests, behavior and much more via Facebook Ads

Cons:

The most competitive social media site especially for small companies. It can be difficult to be noticed by potential clients.

* Strictly controlled for advertisers who have high costs per visit (CPC)

* Not a suitable platform for B2B businesses.

* It can be difficult for novice marketers to get into Facebook advertisements or to navigate the interface.

Tips to Use Facebook for business

Make use of Facebook's site as well as the ad manager or ads library in order to find out how to set up your campaign.

Try different advertising formats to figure out which one is best for your company.

• Join Facebook along with the other popular social media platforms so that you can cross-promote products and other content.

* Take advantage of Facebook Ads' demographic targeting options, including age, gender, interests/behaviors/likes, to focus on the most relevant customers.

* Make use of lead ads on Facebook to gather the contact details of customers who are interested.

* Ensure that your company is active on Instagram, Messenger, and WhatsApp because of their large user count.

2. Instagram

By 2021 Instagram could have 1.69 billion active users per month. It's particularly popular among millennials as well as the female segment, which makes the majority of your small business's potential clients. It is also a popular tool for marketers to utilize it to communicate their message to the world, as photos as well as videos posted on Instagram get more attention than other kinds of content. People also share photos and videos with families and friends and that's why Instagram can be an effective tool for marketers.

Pros:

* Great for B2C marketing since people are Instagram Instagram in order to connect with their favourite brands and to get ideas for the latest products

Great platform for storytelling using images that focuses on the emotions of people

* Helps you connect with the largest number of people that has a specific interest, particularly via social media influencers

It lets you determine the demographics of your customers such as interests, preferences and more via Instagram Ads

Cons:

Cost per Click is higher than the other clicks.

Its algorithms favor accounts that post more times per day. This is not easy when you're just beginning your business.

* It can take a while before people begin to notice your posts appear on their feeds.

* Instagram doesn't permit advertisers to create campaigns that use negative keywords. This is an issue for advertisers looking to eliminate irrelevant traffic.

Strategies for using Instagram for Business

* The most effective strategy for this social media platform is to connect it to other accounts on social media and posting the same content on several platforms. This will allow you to gradually increase your user base.

Create an unambiguous brand voice and analyzing your customers' preferences, behaviors and demographics. You can then determine what type of content you can publish on Instagram to get more effective outcomes.

* Try out various ads to find out the one that is most effective for you and your company.

* Make use of Instagram Stories to show behind-the-scenes footage of your business , to make a stronger relationship with your clients.

Visit Instagram's official app or website to sign up for an account, purchase advertisements to learn more about how Instagram works and familiarize yourself with its functions.

3. LinkedIn

Because LinkedIn boasts more than 530 million users registered and is a fantastic way to reach individuals with specific career preferences and needs. This is great for B2B companies that wish to reach professionals currently in the workforce or who plan to leave their jobs in the near future. This also lets you reach out to customers based on geographical area, which is crucial for businesses trying to remain local. For instance local restaurants could target potential customers in the region who are searching for a restaurant.

Pros:

* Work well when combined with B2B marketing, as B2B marketing is where professionals meet to network and exchange ideas on their respective industries.

* Allows you reach people based on their interests, their location of are employed, their skill sets and other pertinent information

* Great for focusing on specific job titles or positions that you are looking to connect with.

It's so easy to find options for targeting that it's simple to become super-specific in your approach

Cons:

* You cannot post any type of content to this site because the users are there to fulfill professional requirements. If you make an unrelated or offensive advertisement it will have a difficult time getting people to take interest in your company.

* As the target audience is very particular, it requires an enormous amount of planning and effort to identify the people you want to connect with.

The features of LinkedIn are more complicated than other social media platforms It takes time to master the art of making the most of its features.

Strategies for using LinkedIn as a BusinessNetwork:

Prepare your company's details prior to time so that you can have an official website set up in a short time.

* Make sure that your content is geared towards professionals However, don't be scared to post news related to your industry or share some fun occasional posts to keep your readers interested.

* Make use of LinkedIn Pulse to post content created by influential people in your field to draw more attention for your business.

Create an official LinkedIn profile created to make yourself easily available to colleagues. Make use of your LinkedIn profile to share amazing content to aid in the growth of your business.

4. Twitter

Twitter is an online social network that is perfect to reach a large audience of people who are eager to stay up-to-date with most recent news and happenings. This makes it ideal for B2B businesses that want to build connections within their field. It also lets you make ads targeted based on geographic area, making it a great option for local companies. Additionally, Twitter has a wide population of users in 2021. It has more than 330 million active monthly users, which makes it an excellent platform to gain publicity for your business.

Pros:

It allows brands to converse with their customers in real-time , if there are any concerns or issues

* Twitter is a great platform for B2B businesses as its users are generally attracted by information and updates on their particular industry.

* Twitter is more casual in look than LinkedIn it is an ideal choice to B2B companies that wish to appear professional, however, they also want to show an authentic face.

* Ideal for sharing news and information that changes frequently.

Twitter is widely regarded to be one of the most effective platforms for online retailers since it's easy to post information regarding sales or new products, discounts and even announcements

Cons:

Since this site has an informal style, it's easy to get caught in the crossfire and publish things that are offensive or offensive that may cause offence to users and damage your image as a brand.

* Due to its short postings, Twitter doesn't allow for enough space to include any additional details or marketing material that could generate interest in your company.

* Twitter does not work well when you're targeting hyper-specifically since your target audience won't be in a position to locate your content unless they're using hashtags or other keywords that relate to your business.

Tips to Use Twitter for an Enterprise

Maintain a casual tone however professional. This platform is ideal for quick updates about your company since it's not a good platform for long-form content.

* Create a community of people who are interested in your industry and business by making use of hashtags or keywords

relevant to your field to gain more attention.

* Use Twitter Ads If you are looking to gain rapid exposure for your latest items, deals, or discounts. This allows you to focus on users who are fascinated by certain topics and are likely to purchase.

5. YouTube

The video-sharing platform YouTube doesn't need an introduction. YouTube is, in fact, the second largest search engine used today which makes it an ideal platform to share videos for B2B companies looking to attract more customers. It's also among the most well-known platforms for marketing via social media as a whole since its users tend to pay more attention to images such as product demonstrations and instructional videos. Since the platform is mostly focused on videos, it's best utilized by companies that have products or services that they want to showcase.

Pros:

* YouTube is often the most effective places for marketers to access video content that

can bring more subscribers, views and even conversions.

* This is a popular social media platform that is widely known which makes it ideal for companies who want to increase the visibility of their brand.

* Lets you upload hyper-specific videos to an exclusive audience who are interested in all types of content and formats you upload.

Cons:

* YouTube isn't the best choice for news content because it takes a long time to make a video before you can upload it. Your brand could be left out of major opportunities when there are deadline-sensitive announcements such as announcements of new products and deals.

Because the majority of YouTube's content is videos, businesses seeking social media visibility must put their time and effort into making captivating videos that viewers be drawn to.

Tips to Use YouTube for Business

• Post tutorials and product demos in order to attract your customers with pictures that they can easily comprehend.

Make use of this site to post announcements for your business as well as press releases on the latest products and deals and sales. This is the most efficient method to get the word quickly, without the need to make a video in the first place.

Utilize YouTube's search function to locate people who are looking for videos that are related to your company or brand Then, engage them by responding to their comments or initiating conversations.

6. TikTok

This app became an important social media competitor in the year 2018. The majority of its users are Gen Z and millennials interested in short video clips. It is ideally utilized by companies looking to connect with younger consumers However, it could be useful for sharing original content, as the audience likes things which stand out from typical status updates and tweets.

Pros:

It's an online platform that teens typically use, which is why it's great for reaching out to potential customers, or showcasing how awesome your brand is.

If you're searching for ways to reach out to an audience that is younger. If so the social media platform allows you to publish videos of 15 seconds which will be far more engaging than typical text or image posts.

* Users of TikTok are naturally drawn to different kinds of content because they're accustomed to short, entertaining videos such as comedy sketches and music. So, you don't have to fret about spending much time editing your content or making sure that it adheres to the correct structure.

Cons:

* TikTok is only popular with users younger than 24 This means it's not the best location for businesses who need to increase their brand's visibility across various age groups.

* As a lot of young people utilize this platform, there's not enough demand for content that is business-related. Your posts are likely to not be noticed unless they're videos designed for business.

Tips to use TikTok for an Business

Make use of this application to show behind-the-scenes footage from your business, product demonstrations or tutorials that are brief enough to be watched in 15 minutes.

* Connect with people who make fun videos so that your brand's image appears more transparent.

* Post exclusive deals or giveaways to increase your social media presence while not focusing on posts themselves.

Businesses must be active on various social media platforms because their customers may not necessarily use the same platform. That means that if you aren't using one particular app or site and you'll end up getting behind and missing the chance to interact with existing as well as potential customers. Although it may be difficult to manage these platforms, keep in mind that each has each one with a distinct purpose, so you should try to concentrate on a couple of platforms which have the most impact. If you are just beginning with your first social media account Keep track of posts that are successful so that you can reuse them for future campaigns. The longer you commit to making content, the higher chances of getting noticed online.

Chapter 9: Power Of Failure

Failure is a term that frightens a lot of people, particularly in the field of business. Nobody starts an enterprise with the intention of failing, however the probability of failure is higher in the business world than you may imagine. 20% of companies fail within the first year following their initial launch thirty percent fail during the second year, fifty percent fail within five years 70% fail within the 10th year after they started. With these numbers it is easy to believe that it's not worthwhile? However, there are a lot of reasons that lead to the demise of businesses and not all failures are exactly the same. What are the best methods to deal with failures utilized by entrepreneurs? The key is to handle failures being aware that not all types are all created equally. Perhaps, for instance, the hypothesis you test-driven did not result in the way you'd have liked it to be. Therefore, you devise an entirely new method to test the hypothesis , and then learn on the results of the tests you've made previously.

5.1 Every Failure is Different

You must be aware of the various types of failures and how important it is to accept failures in the business world. It is important to understand that certain failures are a part of the process however, some may lead you to the wrong business path. Knowing the value of failing at work can help you in trying out different ways of doing business that you might not to try without. This will enable you reach your full potential. What's the real cause of small-scale businesses failing? They certainly aren't deliberately doing this. A professor from the business school Harvard categorizes business failures into three categories: unavoidable intellectual, preventative, and failures.

The 3 Kinds of Failure

Preventable Failure

The first type of failure is preventable. kind of failure. It's defined as deviations from the specifications in the well-defined procedures for regular or high-volume manufacturing or service operations. If properly supported and trained employees are able to follow these procedures consistently. If they're not lacking the ability, then deviation or inattention is the cause of the failure. These situations can be addressed by using solutions that are easily created. Technically speaking, avoidable failures happen because you aren't following the correct procedure and paying attention to the details or don't have the skills to complete the task. These errors are usually part of everyday routines, such as missing sales calls and typos or even poor feedback from customers. What do you do about preventable mistakes that are large enough to cause disruption but get hidden until it's too late? In the case of many instances, errors of a preventable nature start with the lack of research, planning and planning.

A company didn't have enough capital prior to its start-up, and didn't meet the expectations of its annual revenues. Now , they're in an dispute with investors.

Another company erred on the side of generalization while looking for a phase of market. They began without a complete picture of the market in their minds, not being aware of the buying behaviors of their intended customers, and not focusing the target audience in a proper manner. Then they're losing all their funds to try and make an impact on everyone on the market that is a unclear way to approach things.

A different example is one company that came up with pricing strategies that were unclear and now spends the majority of its time offering discounts and testing promotions. The only way to solve this is to develop an effective pricing strategy designed correctly.

Unavoidable Failures

Failures that are complex or inevitable can be difficult to identify. You've got the protocols as well as the tools and know-how to complete the task, however, something isn't adding to. The combination of external influences and internal distractions play an important role in the complexity of failures.

Here are some of the ways complex failures occur:

* Natural disasters

The best strategies for success are complex and therefore easy to make mistakes.

* The death of an individual leader

* Rapid expansion

The business environment is chaotic , and this could lead to errors

* Leadership is growing

Emergency departments are place to develop a range of inexplicably failings. The hospital is equipped with the staff necessary to perform the task and has procedures to deal with a range of situations it is also equipped (nearly) all the equipment needed to help patients in need of assistance.

If fast-paced situations are entangled by the influx of patients malfunctioning medical equipment, or even atypical or highly sophisticated medical requirements, an inevitable failure will occur. In a world that everyone is well-equipped to handle any situation that may arise unexpected events can occur, and failure is inevitable.

Intellectual Failures

As stated above that not all failures are not created equal. While some of the mistakes can be detrimental to company and are preventable while others are essential, healthy, and can result in huge and fruitful bundles of growth.

Failure is an integral element of learning healthy and taking risks. Failures in the intellectual realm can provide opportunities for new and exciting knowledge , as well as beneficial feedback. This could help increase the effectiveness of the company over the long term. The model of trial and error is the most effective illustration of this kind of failure. What can you do to arrive at the right answer If you don't attempt it repeatedly?

Exploring ideas that are novel and testing the validity of recent hypotheses are all examples of failures in intelligence. Failure could be the outcome in either case, but the process will not be negative due to these failures. You're learning what ideas work and which aren't by experimenting with new ideas and hope that the next time have a better result. Do you believe Thomas Edison got the light bulb just right on the first try? That's certainly not the scenario. He tested a variety of metals before settling on the one that met the requirements and was flawless If this was an example of intellectual development that you have, you could also use it in your thoughts.

A lot of people will offer tips when you're trying to establish an enterprise from scratch. However, I can assure you that very few will advise that you shouldn't make a lot of mistakes. They'll likely tell that you should take risks and not hesitate. However, they won't make an argument in the business world about this attitude's advantages over others in business, and what it does to make you more powerful and sets your company on the path of success in the coming years.

5.2 You're Probably Never Really Winnable If You're Never Failing at All

It might seem odd to some however it's the most significant element of this list according to me. It's an example of how to tackle your tasks. If everything you do is running smoothly, you're not taking enough risks that's why you're not trying to achieve huge wins which will make you stand out significantly even if you're making small wins each day.

You can also be sure that you're not gaining knowledge.

We recognize that we do not know everything. That's why we're always looking for new perspectives that challenge our assumptions and trust evidence to confirm our gut intuitions. We also recognize that when everyone is empowered to bring their own perspective to the table regardless (particularly!) when it results in people not agreeing with us, we'll make better business decisions. The rapid growth we've experienced wouldn't be possible had we not been constantly studying the thoughts of others testing the ideas we thought might work, and then tweaking according to what we discovered.

Rejoice in the failure and then discuss it

It's much more straightforward to talk about failure in a hypothetical way opposed to accepting it. The process of highlighting mistakes when they occur helps to ensure that this mentality ends up becoming an integral part of the culture you're building. So, creating a space where failures are shared openly without hesitation offers the team with the opportunity to learn and helps improve the performance for the future.

It may be daunting to certain people however there are a couple of rules to be followed to ensure that you're following the procedure properly: First, you must know when the process should start (if the team's younger members hear their supervisors discussing the possibility of failure They'll be more inclined to believe that they could, also) Then, it should happen frequently (rather rather than waiting until the "correct moment" to hold a serious discussion) and thirdly and lastly, it must be communicated in a manner that is focused and individual initially (it doesn't matter how you'd prefer to provide feedback however, it's about how the person will be able to receive it in a way that is beneficial to them) And lastly it must be shared.

Chapter 10: Is A Team Necessary?

Business owners typically prefer to handle everything by their own, but eventually they are at a point when they are able to consider the possibility of forming an organization. It doesn't matter if you have a small tech company or retail business hiring employees comes with many challenges as well as advantages. Finding employees who are right fit to be hired in the right time can propel your company to new levels. But, hiring employees that are not the best fit for the task at the wrong time can result in the negative effect and ruin your company. It is important to consider the potential and limitations when you build an organization while trying to make the right decision for your company.

6.1 You Should Ask Yourself"the Famous Five "W" Questions

Who do you want to employ? It may appear to be something that is easy to answer however, many people fail to think about it even. What kind of person would be ideal for the job that you're providing? What do they have in their resumes as well as what exactly are their qualities you're looking for in the candidate you're trying to recruit? What are the aspects that you could make compromises on or what's the aspects that you must not give up completely? It is important to refine your expectations before you begin looking for the right person suitable for the job. Create a single-page document that explains the type of person you're looking for and be as detailed as you can. Beware of the famous "I'll recognize it when I notice the signs" mentality at all at all. If you aren't sure the meaning behind it most likely to never come across it.

What do you anticipate from the the person you're planning to hire? Small-scale business owners have to perform a variety of tasks, from top-level work to administrative tasks. They typically seek an individual who can fulfill some of the duties. This is logical from the point of viewpoint of an entrepreneurial. My job is vast and encompasses almost everything. My employees must be able to perform all of this as well. This is what an entrepreneur might think. But the reality is that it's not their business for which they are required to fulfill all of the tasks. You must have a specific purpose for every person you choose to hire and the job they are assigned must be tailored to their needs. If you are hiring someone for the job of accountant, do not expect them to be able to do the responsibility of creating the brand, as well as creating leads. Many people who are looking to join a startup would like to be in a more relaxed environment and a more relaxed environment, your job is to support them in their growth.

Where can you find your employee? Once you have a clear understanding of the job of the candidate you wish to employ, you must to look for the ideal candidate. There are a variety of options to help you in the process of finding a job however, your network is often your most effective tool. If you're aware of it is true or not, your network could only a few degrees away from making the perfect job. Conduct some research about the people that you already know on the network prior to posting ads online or hiring an employee. LinkedIn is a great starting point but don't limit your efforts to one media platform. Create a distinct web page for your site with information about the position and then share it with social media platforms such as Facebook, Twitter, & Google Plus. You never know who might find the job through the network of friends and then decide to apply.

It's possible that you need someone to work this week however that doesn't mean that it's the best moment to hire. When you expand your team, you will be taking on many new operational and financial obligations. It is possible that you will have to pay higher taxes, purchase insurance or adjust your financials depending on the way you structure the work. Since the rules differ from one place to another location, it's generally best to speak with an accountant or a lawyer prior to beginning the process. It is important to keep in your mind that when you hire an employee, you're no longer just an entrepreneur, you're now an administrator. In addition to basics training you'll also be accountable for managing your staff which will increase the burden. This is why it's crucial to approach hiring from a strategic perspective rather than solely based dependent on the current needs at the start. Deciding when to hire someone is as important as hiring the individual.

Also, you must understand the reason you're creating an organization. Finding the motive behind decisions is typically the most challenging part of the process. But, it can also be the most satisfying and enjoyable aspect. Why do you want to go out to create a team? Are you seeing rapid expansion in your company which requires more structured management? Are you tired and having too many things to do to handle on your own? There may be other motive to think about thoroughly before forming your team. This will allow you ensure that your choice to form an organization is the right one.

When you're capable of answering these questions and answer them, you will find that the "how" will begin to appear slowly. When the "how" begins to reveal itself then there will be numerous other challenges to tackle.

Independent contractor vs. Employee

The hiring process is different for businesses today in comparison to how it was a decade ago. You can manage a full business from anywhere with employees located in different parts of the nation. The days of bringing all your employees under one roof are falling away , and allowing for new methods of doing business. The roles of workers and entrepreneurs change and evolve with the changes in the world of work. Businesses are looking for independent contractors , rather than employing full-time employees. It is possible to define an independent contractor as someone who is willing to perform the task of another according to his own method and methods. Lawyers and accountants are good instances of an independent contractor. There is no requirement to contribute social security tax or withhold taxes on income when you choose to work as an independent contractor over employees who are full-time. You do not have to pay unemployment tax or Medicare. There is no risk of certain types of liabilities and you don't have to pay for any benefits, either. But, you need to recognize that the position of a contractor comes with limitations of its own. The freelancer is free to refuse or accept a job. A freelancer has the ability to take the power to manage their own work. In one way this can help to cut costs However, in the meantime you could face issues which you do not want face. This type of hiring works for certain jobs, but isn't suitable for other positions.

Attracting amazing people

The lifeblood of your business is the staff you choose to hire. They're not just those who you spend most in your working hours, they're also the face of your business. When you're looking to recruit an employee on a full-time basis or employ an independent contractor, you'll want to select the most suitable candidate to do the job. In the end you'll have to determine the type of compensation package you're able to provide and how to present your candidate prior to. In the end, outbidding your competition isn't your only way to attract the best talent. In fact, the fact that you're a startup could give you an edge because many people are attracted by the excitement and potential that a startup offers. Actually, the ability to offer a unique and satisfying working experience is usually your most effective selling point. There are additional methods you can use to attract outstanding people as described below.

Design a catchy job title. What's the motivation to create it? You might be thinking! It's nothing and everything simultaneously. It's a fact you will not be able to give your employee the same amount of benefits as a more established company. Therefore, you can compensate the gap in your budget by being more imaginative with the job titles. If, for instance, you're looking for an associate in sales and your capability to provide the worker with 60% of what the managers of a different business are offering it is possible to play with words and name it the role of a senior sales director. This won't have any affect on you, but someone who is searching for a job might think it's a big change. This will make him feel valued and will help him find an improved job in the near future. Employ names as bargaining chips in order to get workers of higher quality.

146

Long hours of work with no compensation is common in the initial period. Giving attractive incentives to your employees is among the most effective strategies to reduce the stress. Numerous companies have had great satisfaction by offering tiny little, thoughtful benefits for their employees, which range from free lunches and laundry pickup to frequent trips, and subsidised gym memberships.

However, surely, someone can see that a gym membership for free isn't worth a lot less than $10,000 in terms of annual income? This is possible, but not the main point. Numerous studies indicate that money isn't necessarily the most important factor in people's search for new opportunities, especially for younger people. Small rewards can make you stand out and show your appreciation to your employees. Even if you own small-sized company, there are plenty of ways to avail discounts on local services for groups. To receive better discounts it's possible to create a partnership with other business owners in the area. It will put you in greater position to negotiate with more people working for you.

It is important to provide your employees with opportunities to grow. People today don't wish to do the same tasks every day with the same set rules. Instead, they prefer to be in the middle of new challenges every single day to improve and become an expert worker. Your employees can be provided with opportunities to grow and develop that are affordable and permit them to grow into more professional professionals. You can organize learning events or offer scholarships in conjunction with local education programs , or provide experts to meet for employees on their own that assist them in developing their abilities. This will demonstrate to your employees that you are committed to their professional growth This will help them appreciate their work for you. They'll be more committed and excited about their work. These incentives can be useful for those who are new entering your business However, the most effective weapon is the character of your business. The company culture you create at work is superior to these benefits.

6.2 In The Lead

Think about being in the role that of an accountant. The job you have now is simple and easy. You're required to review and keep track of financial records. If you were in a room with entrepreneurs and demanded them to describe their business in one phrase, you'd receive laughter at best. If your business is changing and growing each day, you'll need to grow and evolve while growing. Let's say you've created a service or product after spending a significant amount of time in the beginning phase of your company, and it's now at an conclusion. You now need to consider the management and long-term strategy concerning the direction the company will take. It may sound like a good thing, as the most important thing has been done. For some business owners it can be a challenging change. Based on the character of your business there may be a need for you to oversee a group consisting of just a few people or even 100 people employed by your business. It is essential to build abilities to lead in any situation regardless of the number of people you will have to be under your supervision.

The subject of leadership is a constant discussion that encompasses a myriad of methods and theories that each have their unique advantages and challenges. Find your local bookstore to find books that deal with leadership and you'll discover a myriad of titles with this title. This is also the case for online searches. You can find millions of search results, and there's plenty of information about this subject that one approach will be in opposition to the other. Therefore, it is important to remember that there's not a single method to be a leader at all times. It's not about determining if your style of leadership is good or not. It is more important to be aware of which style of leadership is most effective and which is less efficient. Certain people favor a strict and structured approach when taking charge, whereas other people prefer an inclusive and open approach to leadership.

New generation leaders

You must understand the job an employee has to perform in the present time and age. Their role is different from one of years back. This will enable you determine what kind of leadership style is more efficient. Many dreamed of attending school 50 years ago, and obtaining a job that would allow them to rise up the corporate ladder to eventually retire with a hefty pension. The path to success that appears smooth and organized has gone out of the fashion. The people are searching for jobs that allow them to show their true self. They want a place that allows them to be deeply connected. Maybe that's the very reason you decided to start this business. With the expectations of work changed, the position that a leader plays has changed. The rigid management structure isn't effective as it once was. It is clear that the days of authority within corporate culture are ending and opening the way for a new leader culture that is built on inspiration and influence contrasted to assertion and authority. A great leader isn't identified by a lack of control nowadays. It is instead determined by the degree to which you are able to empower your employees. What does that mean to you as a small company owner and Entrepreneur? How do you work effectively as an executive? This is a huge debate However, there are some guidelines that are applicable to all kinds of leaders.

Genuineness: Employees are looking to their leaders to show the same integrity and transparency that their customers want from the businesses they trust. It's not necessary to know everything in order to be a great leader. It's much more crucial for an individual leader to be genuine in his words and to be transparent about his strengths and weaknesses. There's a reason that your team is yours. They don't only believe in your business; they also trust your abilities. You can reward their trust and respect by promising to act with integrity even when it's a difficult choice.

The ability to adapt It is an ever evolving, and disruptions are occurring in greater and more extensive manners than it has ever been. What works now might not be the same next year. Being flexible and adaptable is essential to being a leader who is effective. You should never depart from your goal or fundamental guidelines. Your business would fail in the absence of these principles. With the constant changes, however you can't remain inflexible or static. A single size doesn't fit every situation, and it's your responsibility to create an approach that is adaptable.

Accountability: Some think that in the role of leadership, you have to appear confident and strong and never admit you've committed a mistake out of fear of being perceived as weak or insecure. This was the case to the old days, but it's not the case anymore. Leaders of today must be held accountable for the decisions they make. The bad ones as well as the positive ones are included. It is important to look at the world of pop culture to get more clarity about this. What's the most embarrassing way that politicians, celebrities, and business leaders could do when they make mistakes in public? The answer is blame another person. One of the initial motives is to blame another person or group and avoid the responsibility. This can lead to more disasters. You become human in the role of an executive when you accept the responsibility for your actions which caused a problem. People become more enthused about the organization as a result of this.

They begin to respect your company. Every person makes mistakes, and you're likely to make them. It's up to you to confront them. If you don't your position as a leader could be extremely short.

Accessibility: Some circles believe that being available all of the time is a problem. They argue that if everybody is able to access you, it erodes your standing as an individual leader. However, being unaccessible isn't a true indicator of superiority. Instead, it indicates that you're out of contact. We have become accustomed to instant feedback in the modern world. Platforms for communication like text messages or email as well as social media has made access simple these days. It is a difficult alternative. Many employees don't want in waiting until they receive a formal evaluation about their achievements. The public needs information instantly. Politicians are expected to adopt Facebook and Twitter as well as the top executives of corporations are expected to write blogs. It is imperative to be open-minded from the operational and philosophical standpoint as a leader in the present. If you examine every one of these areas you will discover that they all share one incredible thing in common. These qualities are those that people are looking for from friendships that are personal. Every person wants a flexible and genuine friend, don't they? Every person wants your loved ones to be easily accessible and accountable.

Personal and professional expectations have been treated separately for many years, however, they are beginning to blend gradually. The distinction between work and life is gradually disappearing as are our expectations for each. These concepts start to become clearer as you begin to realize that the personal and professional aspects of our lives are becoming one. This isn't a generational change or a trend that is new. It is rather an era of leadership where these traits are essential.

6.3 What kind of leader Are You?

If you look at your role as a leader, and then evaluate your business by others and organizations to draw inspiration from is an obvious thing to do. I would like my products to be as successful as the ones of Nike or to be as successful as Jeff Bezos. This is a great beginning point, but it is only the beginning the journey.

Being a leader of high quality isn't something one can order from your favorite restaurant, and then say "I'll buy whatever she's having." It's more like an open buffet. So, it is important to recognize what you require and then discipline yourself in the right way. In the event that you don't, your life will become messy.

If you were to ask the CEO of a large business what his preferred style of leadership is, you wouldn't receive a clear answer. So, it's not essential to follow the same type of leadership However, it is important to be aware of the traits that are most efficient in accomplishing specific tasks.

I'll discuss 7 most popular leadership styles. You are able to ask yourself which best suits your business and you. Also, you don't have to adhere to one fashion every day and forget about the others. The aim is to look at all options available and blend them into an aesthetic that matches your tastes.

Democratic Leaders who are democratic believes that the decision-making process as a collective decision. Instead of asking a single group or individual to make decisions the leader asks the entire group to be involved. This is a popular and efficient method of leading because it makes everyone feel respected and heard. However, it does have its negatives. This type of leadership can lead to confusion and disorganization within the workplace, which leads to confusion and poor communication. This type of leadership is ideal for smaller companies with all employees of the same level.

Leadership that is authoritarian may be the first thought that comes into mind when people imagine a relationship between a leader and follower. Leaders who follow this model tend to make decisions independently. You're likely to be familiar with this kind of leadership if been under the control of a boss who enjoys micromanaging his job. Don't dismiss it at this point. It's more of a continuous process than one shade. Not all authoritarian leaders are able to misuse their power or turn into vicious rulers. This is a good choice in an environment in which the leader has more knowledge than others on the team , or when it is imperative to make decisions quickly regularly.

Leaders who are transformational: thinking, and more talk are typical characteristics of leaders who are transformational. They're praised for their ability to inspire and motivate others to succeed. They're known for their enthusiasm and determination and can see the best in people. They place the quality of their behavior over anything else. While this type of leader could be a great asset to the company, it is essential to surround him with people who are organized and focused. If not, the leader's greatest ambitions may be nothing greater than the idea of. This is a good thing for a business that is dependent on innovation to thrive.

Laissez-faire: This kind of leadership seeks to concentrate on each individual and ask them for their opinion and offering guidance alongside. It involves a lot of apathy, and research suggest that it's one of the most ineffective ways to guide a group.

It's ideal in an organization that have a high-performing team.

Servant: This style of leadership is dedicated to helping people achieve their potential to the fullest extent. The leader shares their power with their team members and puts an enormous amount of time to develop the professional skills of the team members. The team is still a main management team whose job is to help people develop and flourish. The ideal fit is for businesses with the pursuit of a particular goal.

The type of leader emphasizes structure, organization and a clearly defined chain of command since they believe that employees must be penalized or compensated in proportion to their performance. A leader who is transactional also puts an emphasis on processes, rules and procedures, and expects other employees to do the same. This type of leader is typically appreciated as things go smoothly and performance is good. However, be cautious when things begin to go wrong! The leader of transactions believes that errors and mistakes should be punished swiftly and decisively. The transactional leader is more effective in certain kinds of teams than others and it can have an positive and negative effect on the business. It's a good fit for traditional companies with a solid middle-level management.

Affiliation: A leader attaches the greatest importance to his people. He is more concerned with emotions than performance. The actions taken by an executive focus on providing his team with harmony and a sense of comfort when they be part of a team. The majority of his work is directed toward fostering collaboration and connections within his team. This kind of leader can add value to the organization, however, their natural aversion to conflicts can cause issues. This kind of leader is appropriate for businesses that are focused on improving the culture at the workplace and boosting the morale of their employees.

6.4 sharing the load

Whatever type of leadership style you decide to adopt however, one thing is certain: you will need to trust others with the task of doing it correctly. Entrepreneurs spend many hours making, setting up, and expanding their business, so it's very difficult for them take on the responsibility of other employees. They do not want anyone else to be in any way under control because they are afraid that the company's direction might not be the direction they wish them to go. But knowing when to distribute the burden and how to accomplish it is an essential aspect of the success of a leader.

In order to accomplish this effectively, you must abandon the notion that a leader has total control of everything at all times. From managing to inventing the environment, many people believe that a the leader should have the entire control. However, this isn't an actual fact. An effective leader has the obligation of laying the company's vision however, he is not required to implement everything during the process. Whatever your abilities are, there will always be certain weaknesses that can be compared to your strengths. This is good since it lets you determine what you can handle on your own and what you can't. This means that you can hand over the tasks to someone others and focus on doing most effectively. This approach is not just to aid you in your role as an executive, but will benefit your company all-around. You're not simply assigning work to someone else however you show confidence in the person you are affirming that you trust the person. This improves the morale of those working for you , and encourages an environment of confidence and instigation. If you're not sure about delegating work for someone else start by delegating the burden of something that's less significant. For instance, instead of giving over the financials of your company, you could share an easy task that will not affect the business as much in case it fails. Let the person in charge handle the task on their own, without interference and as you begin to see people tackling new tasks efficiently it will give satisfaction and enable you to divide larger tasks with other people. This will allow you to have more time to utilize to concentrate on the overall idea of the business.

Chapter 11: Making Your Message Heard

Who would like to know more about investment products while cleaning the kitchen floor. But do you have the funds to invest? Holden wonders. In the end, reaching an impressive quality of reach means selecting the right medium and scheduling commercials at the proper timings. The aim of frequency is giving viewers a sufficient amount of time to allow the message to be absorbed within the many distractions of everyday life. The impact of the message is what it is. Your message should be compelling enough to cut through the multitude of distractions clients face on a regular basis. Furthermore, it should be presented at the appropriate time.

7.1 Communication

Media advertising

Above-the-line marketing has three primary purposes: to inform to remind and persuade the people who are watching you about your products as well as services. The amount of revenue you could create per cent you spend for advertising can be a amount of the cost for advertising. Film advertisements can assist a local eatery in attracting late-night patrons. Advertising on on public transportation could help an agency to recruit as it can be seen by thousands of people in the appropriate groups every day. Local radio has proven to be an effective and cost-effective method for small businesses.

Non-media communications

The communication through non-media platforms offers many possibilities and is most often accessible to companies that are just beginning to develop. Sales literature is one tool that is popular and comprises glossy brochures, as well as products fliers that are one sheet. They can be dropped through the letterbox, or placed in the windscreen wipers of a car's windshield. They may also be sent directly. The messages should focus on a particular target audience and should highlight the most important advantages of the product and its advantages. The most effective method for advertising is direct marketing, in which all types of marketing are accepted, and the customer is expected to respond directly to an advertiser rather than having to go through an agent or retailer. This can include telephone sales as well as direct mail too. It is also beneficial to develop an online presence for your company. Finding someone to design and build simple websites shouldn't cost much but keeping it simple is the best option as too complex websites could be a turnoff to potential customers. You could even create one on your own as there are many programs that will help you with the process. If you're planning to develop your own website, you'll need to notify your customers that your site is available online. The response rate can be tracked, which is among the many advantages of under-the-line marketing as opposed to traditional advertising. It is nevertheless important to remember that a return percentage of 2% to 3% is considered as normal, while 5 percent is a good rate while 0% is a sign that something is seriously off. Buy three curries , and get one for free in the following week, for instance. it could be used to promote sales and point of sale in order to give customers an additional incentive and build loyalties. This also comes with the benefit of stopping competition. This type of offer can be made in the store at point of sale, or through mail drops. They're an ideal way to help start-ups begin its journey. Sponsorship can be a valuable tool too. Are there local nurseries or community-based initiative within your locality that could need equipment? It is possible to donate the equipment in exchange for a contract in which your business receives publicity. When the reason is worthy this could result in positive word-of mouth support. Be careful not to create overly hyped about your donation as well as the generosity as it could be perceived as shady and unwise.

Public relations

Pr is viewed as a variety of things, but the most important thing is it is considered to be an element that allows a business to reach out to its customers in a truthful and exact way. This includes launches of products as well as media releases and openings to premises. You must follow some simple steps to accomplish it. Create an event to launch the event or mail local newspapers with a press release. Look for the best trade journals. Check out the section on business at the library in your area to find the relevant titles. Look through directories of publications to locate trade journals. Contact the publisher and find out who is accountable for covering your area. The goal is to make your press release as easy as you can. Journalists receive hundreds of releases per week, and deadlines are a bit tight. If you write a lengthy press release, it's likely to end up somewhere in the garbage. Be sure to not make big claims.

Make it easy and send the reporter an opportunity to the press conference's opening. It is important to make sure it is not in conflict with the press days. Try to establish an agreement. There may be other details that reporters can use to write an article. You could be eligible for a free plug-in in return. Be aware that the content of editorials in newspapers and magazines carries much more importance for viewers than advertisements. Therefore, take the time to regularly send out press releases, try to locate specific journalists whom you have contacts, provide your services as an educated journalist to publications, propose the writing of a free set of important (and brief) articles, or help sponsor important local events. Though its effectiveness could require years of development and develop, writing letters to editors could be an incredibly efficient marketing strategy.

7.2 Paying Yourself

The motivation behind the idea of starting a business for certain people is to be rich, but less than a quarter of them achieve this. Therefore, you must consider the amount you're paying yourself at the start. At the beginning of the company there is a good chance you'll want to invest all of your money into your business to ensure it has an opportunity to succeed However, in addition to the necessity of saving enough money for running and marketing costs, you need for yourself to have a life. In the beginning, when there is no chance of generating profit will be a challenging period. If you've changed your life away from safety and security of a regular paycheck it is impossible to live without spending a dime. There are financial obligations you must meet along with those that you've accumulated as you pursue the idea of starting an enterprise. So, it is crucial that you have the funds to cover your needs quickly.

If you don't make these decisions on time, you could end up borrowing more or accumulating additional debts on the credit card. This puts you in a situation where you'll be facing more stress. Because when you start your own business is already putting yourself under a lot of stress. So, adding the stress of not having enough money that bothers you even though you're not engaged in the pressure of establishing the business can affect your work you've put many hours into. What is the appropriate amount you need to be able to pay yourself? It is likely to be determined by the industry you're entering and is consequently, the best location to seek out the answers. Engage with others in the industry on a similar level and ask what was that they were paying at the beginning, and where are they now. It is also possible to contact the trade association for assistance when someone from the company isn't willing to assist you. Make a similar estimation of your company's finances and then see if the difference is apparent. If you do not see anything similar, it could be something you're doing incorrectly, or perhaps your entire approach is flawed and you have to deal with the issue before it destroys everything you've been working all day. It is important to plan your actions prior to time so you can spot anything that isn't there. Be sure to pamper yourself every now and then but don't go too far. Don't underestimate your expenses for living, but in the end, you'll prefer to put all of it back to the company. Keep your word about what you must have and include the cost in your budget.

Chapter 12: Management Of Finances Do

You Require Funding?

Infrequently, an entrepreneur has an idea that is brilliant and gets his company in operation. It seems like everything is going well in the first few months. There are some roadblocks and difficulties, but the overall picture appears to be relatively easy. In the midst of nothing it appeared to be an avalanche of issues that weren't even close. They consume many time and resources. The budget gets tighter and the business appears to be off-track. A moment of absolute clarity is spotted and the company is running out of cash rapidly. If you do not come up with an immediate source of income then the business doesn't have the chance to survive.

4.1 Understanding the concept of financing

It's not a true statement however, businesses frequently have to pay for their expenses during the initial stages and then are blown off the market. Lack of planning in this instance is the main reason why many of the best ideas have never been put to market. The enthusiasm and optimism are key factors in the success of entrepreneurs however, only when they are combined with foresight and a sense of.

Every business needs money to start, and, sometimes, a large amount of it. Certain businesses are functioning with a minimum amount of money, while other businesses cannot. Always keep an idea of the costs in the beginning, regardless of the amount of funding required by your company. If you do not, you may end up in a flash, and more importantly, you may become bankrupt. Take a look at the entire financial situation to get an accurate assessment of expenses. There isn't a specific method to determine the cost because the numbers fluctuate based on the status of incorporation as well as the type of business and the location. But you can be aware of the most fundamental expenses that nearly every business has in common.

Inventory is an integral part of your financial plan. Items like raw materials as well as shipping and packaging are all included in this. If you're applying to include the costs of selling commissions, insurance for shipping and warehouse expenses that might be incurred by your company. A majority of these expenses will be repeated over the course of the life of your company.

You must list the prices for professional assistance that is likely to be required to complete your business, such as creating your legal framework. hiring a lawyer, or an accountant, and obtaining trademarks or patents. It is also important to list the permits and licenses, as well as any consultants from outside that might be required. A third part of your expense will be advertising and selling. Business cards, stationery, and other items needed for marketing are covered in this. You'll require someday a website to market the products and services you offer. Everything that is related to marketing such as attending trade shows or conferences that are related to the industry is a must in this section.

Costs of operations: Operations make up a different aspect in your spending plan. It includes everything from utility bills to insurance. Keep in mind that you should include costs such as furniture, internet, rent and administrative requirements parking, office equipment.

Infrastructure is an additional component of your budget, based on the kind of business you're trying to establish. Equipment as well as machinery and other items that are costly to infrastructure depending upon the type of company. Computing-related products, particularly computers are a common every business that exists. Examine the costs for the most common technology items which will be required by your company and put them into your budget.

It is important to keep in mind another factor when you are formulating the cost. It is important to record the single-time costs separately from costs that will continue. The acquisition of basic equipment and the incorporation of the business is in fact only a one-time expenditure, whereas inventory and rent are instances of expenses which will continue running throughout the lifetime of your company.

If you're still uncertain about the costs involved in beginning your business, then you can seek advice from someone who's established a similar business and follow their guidance. An immediate competitor may not be able to assist however, someone who has some differences in their market may be able to help. It is also possible to get assistance on the internet. The best advice is to increase the amount you first estimated, because regardless of how much time you put into calculating the costs, you'll be unable to cover a lot of expenses that might shock you right on the spot. Don't want an unaccounted for expense to ruin all your hard work and planning at the end.

4.2 Financing Your Business

After analyzing all the costs, you will realize that you'll require more money than you thought. It's not something to be disappointed with. There are numerous methods of securing capital regardless of whether you're launching your own small-scale business from your home, or a big company that has many complications. Each method has its own advantages. It's not about the best or worst way to finance your company, but rather which one will best suit your business. You must thoroughly research through your options before settling on one particular method of financing.

The first choice is to finance your business your self, without obtaining cash from other sources. Some of the top entrepreneurs have founded their companies using their own money. The main benefit of this method is that it allows you total control over your company. The only person who cooks on the stove is yourself. However, it can also pose the greatest risk to your personal safety since you could be unable to save your entire savings in the event of a mishap in your business. Smaller startups often have their own ventures funded initially, but seek external help later.

Family members and friends

Another alternative is to borrow capital from friends or family members. This can be a difficult option because if the venture is successful and you make an impressive profit to those closest to you however, if things go in the wrong direction, they'll are liable to lose their entire investment. It is important to consider how you intend to structure the deal prior to giving it to your family and your friends as debt or equity. A person who invests in equity is the proprietor of the business in part , and gets part of the profits. The debt arrangement is a way to ensure that the lender will become a creditor to you and both of you have a contract to repay. Examine both of these arrangements and decide which one fits you the best.

What's the first idea that comes to your head after you hear the term "marketing"? A Facebook page or a brochure for your business? A TV ad? Perhaps you have seen a contest advertisement in Face book or a business advertising on television. These ideas are right as they are all in that category called marketing. However, marketing is not just an organization or a program It's an integral component of all businesses. According to the American association of marketing, a collection of operations and institutions to communicate, create, and exchange of offerings that provide importance to clients, partners, customers and society at large. The bridge that connects customers to your company is known as marketing. It's the string which gives you the chance. There are numerous disputes among entrepreneurs over what method of marketing is the most effective, however they all agree that marketing is essential. You may be thinking about the distinction between advertising, public relations or marketing. This is a difficult issue. Discuss it with professionals in business and you'll get many different solutions. But, those who are entering the industry in the very first instance must be aware of one major differentiator.

Marketing refers to the whole process of communication , not just one specific process. From marketing strategy to media research, think of marketing as an overall communication between company and the client. It's the sum of all interactions with the customer.

Advertising and PR in contrast, are actions that aid in bringing products or services to the market. As an example, an advertisement is a digital purchase or send a letter to the customer. That means that if marketing is the creation of ideas, then advertising and PR are delivery methods. They deliver the service and products to the customer. They are three elements that can stand on their own but are typically part of a larger marketing strategy.

As your company develops and expands, you might require a thorough comprehension of all aspects. Marketing will however be used to explain all the connections linking your company to the outside world throughout this guide.

Embracing your brand

Branding is yet another crucial element that is part in general marketing. Branding is more than a basic product or service. It adds an emotional element to your company. The visual and psychological depiction of the identity of your business. The art of making a symbol, name or design that distinguishes and differentiates your company from other product on the market is the essence of branding. It blends complicated elements like the color scheme, design and logos with abstract elements such as mission goals, values, and goals. These elements, when put together, give your company an overall look that sets it in a different way from other companies. The majority of people don't think of the product they like when they consider it. They react to the sensation that they experience from the product. Imagine the world's most well-known brand around the globe such as Coca-Cola. Are you thinking of carbonated waters as well as brown syrup when hearing the word Coca-Cola? Most likely not. Since if it was the first thought that crossed consumers in their minds the company could be in the red. It is likely that you will think of the refreshing red can when hearing the word Coca-Cola. You might even be able to recall the most beautiful moment that occurred during drinks. This is the one that continues to draw people to drink coke, and not carbonated water, or brown syrup.

It's the same about Apple. Forbes estimated Apple's value with a value of $87 billion, which is 52 percent more than two years back. This is a huge increase. What is the story behind a business that was a homegrown venture become one of the largest companies worldwide? Steve Jobs understood the potential of the brand. He was aware that he needed to infuse the brand into the every aspect of the company and incorporate it into every interaction, just similar to other pioneers. He realized that a strong brand is the most powerful draw to make customers feel loyal because they feel they feel a stronger relationship with the company opposed to simply trading cash with products. Customers feel that they are part of a larger purpose. It's like being an "Apple person" instead of simply hopping through the market and purchasing the top products. Small-scale business owners have a belief that branding is only carried out by big companies that have an enormous amount of money. All you need to do is to be more imaginative to make your product an iconic brand rather than the expenditure of a large sum of money.

You've got a clear vision of your goals within your head, and all you have to do is incorporate the concept into every aspect of your business. What is the one thing you are a firm believer in? What are your goals in all this and what is your background? What is the impression you want customers to feel upon hearing about your business? How do your services and products reflect the larger mission that you've envisioned for your business? When you translate those answers in actions then the brand I'm referring to will begin to emerge. Brands are your most powerful connector and distinctive feature. It's the guarantee you give to each of your clients. So, it is important to not undervalue it.

The preparation for the possibility of

Conclusion

It is important to take seriously the plan you've got in mind to begin a business, in the event that you've come to this point. It is now your decision to make use of this information. You've been taught every step from the beginning to the beginning of a company and the way that markets work. How do you reach your target market and create the culture of your workplace? This is the perfect time to put it into practice and possibly take the pages off to ensure that you're doing the right thing. You shouldn't have any doubt anymore and have everything clearly. You need to have the right mentality to accomplish this because it takes lots of commitment, time energy, and cash. You should have an understanding of how other people have accomplished things around you, and how they've encountered challenges, and devised ways to conquer them to ensure their ideas are successful. This will allow you to manage your business on your own principles. It is also important to be aware that there's likely to be nobody who has ever launched an enterprise without making mistakes when it comes to the method. Failure without success is a term that is not real. Everything is part of the larger picture that makes up success in the end. It is important to tackle your challenges with the proper attitude because they could make or break you.